Brothers in Blood

Tim Brown and Paul Cheston

BLAKE

Published by Blake Publishing Ltd,
98–100 Great North Road, London N2 0NL, England

First published in Great Britain in 1994

ISBN 1 85782 096 7

British Library Cataloguing-in-Publication Data:
A catalogue record for this book is available from
the British Library.

Typeset by Dacorum Type & Print, Hemel Hempstead

Printed by Cox and Wyman, Reading

1 3 5 7 9 10 8 6 4 2

To Inspector Jim Adamson,
the detective who refused to let go.

Contents

Authors' Note

This book was originally intended to be an account of the few detectives who never gave up, those who, with dogged determination, tracked down and brought Roderick and Mark Newall to justice.

There is no doubt that the crucial legal battles were fought out in Gibraltar, in a setting so curiously similar to Jersey. Once both brothers were back in Jersey it was a mere formality to ensure they were sent to prison. It had taken Desmond de Silva QC, heading the Crown team, fifteen months of heavy legal argument to extradite Roderick. And it was on the Rock that the authors found an open atmosphere, conducive to making all the facts available. There was a unique relationship between the press, lawyers and police; it was not unusual to see representatives of all these groups discussing the case long into the night in restaurants and bars. Out of this frankness and conviviality a tacit green light was given to enable this extraordinary story to emerge, with the full facts, to ensure that those who deserved the credit received it.

Once back in Jersey, however, the atmosphere soured

overnight. The warmth of Gibraltar turned into cold officialdom. Senior detectives, previously so open, friendly and encouraging, became introverted and suspicious. Gone was any hope of maintaining co-operation. The authors were therefore forced to switch the focus of their attention. They were officially informed that no member of the Jersey police force could be interviewed about the case. They learned that there were fears at the highest level that out of the Newall case would be created a Bergerac-type character who – as in the TV series – would triumph as a hero, capturing all the glamour and glory at the expense of his superiors.

Such a scenario existed only in the minds of a few powerful figures. It had always been made clear in Gibraltar that the story should and would be told as it happened. There *are* heroes, outstanding people who emerged over the six years, but some have to remain anonymous because of this misguided attitude.

Apart from those names who appear in the following pages, the authors would like to offer their sincere thanks to Dominic Searle, the best newsman on the Rock of Gibraltar; Bill Bond, for 'holding the fort'; Stephen Clackson, for allowing time for investigation; Allan Ramsay, Tom Leonard and also Ed Owen in Madrid for passing on his lucky encounter; the chef at the Royal Hotel, St Helier for helping to track down Paris contacts, and to the many kind people in Jersey who helped in countless ways.

The Players

The victims	**Nicholas Newall**: 56, one-time schoolteacher **Elizabeth Newall**: 47, housewife
Murderer	**Roderick Newall**: then aged 22, former army officer turned ocean-going yachtsman
Accomplice to cover-up	**Mark Newall**: then 21, City financier
Family	**Stephen Newall**: businessman and lecturer, twin brother to Nicholas **Nan Clark**: married to retired police surgeon, sister to Elizabeth
The lawyers	**Desmond de Silva QC**: London barrister, led for the Crown in Gibraltar **Ian Christmas**: legal adviser to States of Jersey police **Cyril Whelan**: chief advocate for the prosecution in Jersey **Christopher Finch**: Gibraltar-based lawyer representing Roderick on Rock **David Le Quesne**: Head of brothers' legal team in Jersey

BROTHERS IN BLOOD

The police **Paul Marks**: former CID chief, now Assistant
Chief Officer in Jersey
Jim Adamson: started inquiry as sergeant, rose
to inspector
Martin Fitzgerald: inspector, headed inquiry in
its last months
Graham Nimmo: CID, now retired
Charles MacDowall: detective sergeant
Louis Wink: inspector, Royal Gibraltar Police

Chronology

11 April 1965	Roderick Newall born in Glasgow, Scotland.
22 June 1966	Mark Newall born in St Andrews, Scotland.
1967	Newall family leave Scotland, arrive in Jersey.
September 1986	Nicholas Newall sells Crow's Nest to Maureen and David Ellam.
10 October 1987	Nicholas and Elizabeth Newall murdered.
May 1988	Roderick resigns from army and sets sail around the world.
Christmas 1989	Roderick leaves New Zealand.
January 1990	Roderick arrives in the Falklands.
February– *April 1990*	Police on Jersey review the case. No new evidence.
January 1991	Nicholas and Elizabeth officially declared dead. The inheritance becomes available. Roderick is in Brazil.
July 1991	Roderick confesses to Helena Pedro.
September 1991	Roderick returns briefly to the Falklands.

May 1992	Roderick and Helena meet Mark in Miami, USA.
June 1992	Roderick returns to London.
July 1992	Roderick confesses to Uncle Stephen at Dunkeld House Hotel, Scotland.
August 1992	Roderick arrested by Jersey detectives aboard HMS *Argonaut*.
November 1992	Gibraltar magistrate almost releases him again.
December 1992	Helena Pedro is brought to Jersey to make statement.
March 1993	Mark is arrested in Paris and extradited to Jersey.
October 1993	Roderick and Jersey authorities agree a deal in Gibraltar.
November 1993	Roderick returns to Jersey and helps police locate the bodies of his dead parents.

Foreword

As Roderick and Mark Newall languished in La Moye prison awaiting sentence over the double murder of their parents, the Jersey Tourist Board launched a massive and expensive publicity campaign to promote the island under the slogan: 'It must be heaven'.

'The Gods have always smiled on the Island of Jersey,' claimed the exuberant copy writers. But even the residents of Valhalla might have balked at having to live in such a controlled society.

The Channel Island consists of forty-five square miles and 84,000 inhabitants, divided into twelve parishes. The fact that the population has exploded by some fifty per cent in the last thirty years indicates the island's popularity and opportunities, but also the need for strict controls. Those controls would not be tolerated in other parts of Europe, although they were necessitated by an acute housing shortage. There is one system of rights for Jerseymen and another for the rest, who include 2,300 Portuguese and more than 10,000 Scots, Irish and English.

No one is allowed to buy property unless qualified by twenty years' residency. Such people are known as 'quallies'. Even birth in the island does not confer the right to settle there, unless there have been ten uninterrupted years of residency. The only housing available for those without these qualifications is often of low quality, but at a very high rent.

If you have real money, however, you can walk straight in. Regulation 1(1)K sees to that. Such applicants are normally expected to be worth at least £10 million and to have a yearly income of £1 million. Applicants have to be interviewed by the all-powerful housing committee, answering questions about their lives, philosophy, ambitions and money. There are some twenty applicants a year, but only about a quarter are successful.

One applicant made headline news when he was unanimously refused the full status of a resident. Actor John Nettles, whose television role as Bergerac made Jersey famous across the world and attracted millions of extra pounds to the island from tourism, found the door barred. There was uproar, appalling publicity and the committee was forced to back down.

What is Jersey's attraction for these millionaires, apart for its stunning scenery and easy living? It is the flat rate of twenty per cent income tax across the board, applying to the lowly potato pickers and the international banking fraternity alike. More than £50 billion is deposited in banks in the island, providing more than half the income for this most attractive tax haven. As might be expected, in this money-minded society, there are radical laws of trading: no new business may be started up without government approval, no business may take on extra staff without permission and at one time there was even a freeze on the creation of new jobs. It is wealthy businessmen who make up the bulk of the political establishment. There are no political parties and each candidate for public office stands on his own platform.

Where Jersey departs most radically from the mainland is in its law enforcement, which is still based in many ways on medieval practices. There are more unpaid and part-time policemen – 300 – than the full-time professionals, who number 240. These honorary officers, known as centeniers, venteniers and constables, have in some ways more power than their professional colleagues. Their strongholds are the villages and parishes, where they have the power to set up roadblocks, make arrests and bring charges. For example both Roderick and Mark Newall, tracked down by the States of Jersey Police CID, had to be formally charged by the centenier for the parish where the crime took place. Officially, states police officers – as a matter of courtesy – are expected to inform the local honorary officer every time they enter his patch on an investigation.

This uneasy relationship between the professionals and the amateurs, which would be considered incredible on the British mainland, has led to calls for a long-overdue, thorough examination of public policing by the Bailiff of Jersey and HM Inspector of Constabulary.

Antiquated and eccentric it may be, but there is no doubt that Jersey is a thoroughly law-abiding society. The police court in St Helier normally deals only with the speeding motorist (the island has a blanket 40-m.p.h limit), the odd drunk, petty thief and other minor miscreants. A low-key raid on a jeweller's shop, netting a few hundred pounds, makes front-page news in the local evening newspaper. Some 666,000 holidaymakers and 135,000 day trippers find a 1950s English setting of decent behaviour in a safe environment.

Vice is almost non-existent. The locals are happy to tell visitors that the only known prostitute who arrived to set up trade had been in her hotel room only for a few hours before she received a knock on the door – not from a client, but from the police, who put her on the next ferry to the mainland.

This is the reason why, when Roderick and Mark carried out their evil crime, the islanders and their police had to struggle to acknowledge that it could have happened at all.

Barely a handful of serious crimes had happened on the island since the German occupation. It had been two decades since there had been a long-running Jersey crime story to dominate the British media. The establishment shuddered. The Tourist Board, which had worried that the fictional violence in 'Bergerac' might scare off potential tourists, feared that the all too real Newall affair would jeopardize the island's image as a haven of safety and tranquillity.

The downside of the 1950s attitude is found in the island's approach to its immigrant workers. The Portuguese are renowned for their readiness to work long hours for low pay in menial jobs which, however essential to the island economy, would never be performed by the residents. The Portuguese are the backbone of the fruit and vegetable industry, worth £27 million a year. And adverts, illegal under race-equality laws in Britain, stating: 'Portuguese housemaid wanted', appear regularly in the local newspaper.

Jersey basks in the Gulf Stream, making it one of the sunniest and warmest spots in Britain; its fifty miles of coastline boast some of the finest beaches anywhere. But this paradise island is not strictly British: it is governed by the locals for the locals.

Roderick and Mark Newall are no longer an embarrassment to the island. They are serving their sentences on the mainland.

1

The Last Supper

It was about 3 a.m. on 11 October 1987. The small hired van sped along the twisting and narrow country lanes of Jersey. Roderick was at the wheel, driving at his usual reckless, breakneck speed. In the passenger seat his brother Mark was trying to calm him. Only a short time before, Roderick had been hysterical, incoherent, cradling a shotgun in his arms and threatening to blow his brains out.

In the back, on the bare floor of the van, lay two dead bodies bound and trussed like mummies in tarpaulin and plastic sheeting.

They hurtled down the hill towards Grève de Lecq, spades and a pickaxe rattling around beside the bodies. Rounding a bend, they saw the lights of a scattering of houses and Roderick realized he had driven too far, so he reversed back up the hill, halting by the side of the road. He threw open the back doors and, with Mark's help, pulled the bodies out and tossed them over the bank and into a field.

Roderick drove the van back to the bottom of the hill and parked in a lovers' layby. He then ran back to help his brother drag the bodies up the gentle grassy slope to the edge of the trees. In the still of the night, while families slept only a few hundred yards away, Mark and Roderick Newall started to dig in an effort to hide their parents for ever.

The day had begun well: Elizabeth Newall had rarely been happier about her family as she sat at her dressing-room table brushing her beautiful red hair. Her boys, Roderick and Mark, had flown over from the mainland to Jersey for a special occasion: her coming 48th birthday.

'The boys have arrived to give me a lovely surprise,' she had told her Portuguese maid, Netti, excitedly that morning.

She knew the family had never been happy together. When the boys had lived at home there had been terrible rows, stand-up shouting matches, in fact, and now they were spread hundreds of miles apart, sometimes at different ends of Europe. But tonight was going to be different. It was her birthday in six days' time and everyone had promised to make a special effort to be nice to one another. Elizabeth, still a strikingly handsome woman, had bought a new outfit, a lovely cream blouse and tartan skirt, from Harrods, where she liked to spend hundreds of pounds in a single swoop. Earlier in the day she had splashed out on an expensive Burberry and a Rolex, before making several purchases at De Gruchy's, the favourite department store of the island's richest residents.

In the lounge, her husband Nick was puffing his pipe and sipping his favourite malt. Even he had made an effort to dress for the occasion, forsaking his normal island wear of open-necked sports shirts and well-worn jerseys in favour of a blue suit. Mark had booked a table at the Sea Crest, the expensive Petit Port restaurant renowned as the best on the island, with its spectacular views over the Corbière lighthouse and rugged cliff walks.

It all seemed so perfect, Elizabeth thought as she joined her husband downstairs.

How could she have known that Roderick, the gallant officer and gentleman, would have murder on his mind before that mild October night was out? Within hours, she and Nick would be bludgeoned to death and, before dawn rose over the holiday island, their bodies would be buried in shallow graves, still in their best clothes.

Mark, the money-minded son, the personification of the booming 1980s City success, drove over from his island home La Falaise, with Roderick, to find two bottles of champagne on ice ready to start the party. Nicholas and Elizabeth both considered themselves 'quality' drinkers, never seen drunk but known to enjoy and appreciate good wines and malts.

An hour later, having finished the champagne, the four arrived at the Sea Crest in Nick's Citroën, to find the car park packed with the usual top-of-the-range cars, reflecting the top-quality clientele. Inside, the restaurant was bubbling. They ordered more drinks in the bar and studied the menu while waiting for their table.

From that moment, Elizabeth's dream of a happy evening began to shatter. Staff quickly sensed the growing tension between the four: Elizabeth's over-loud voice trying to keep spirits up, the cold indifference between Nick and Mark . . . no small talk about army life and City deals here. Showing them to table seventeen in a secluded alcove by the french windows overlooking the bay, their waiter, Duarte Conceicao, soon knew this was no normal family gathering.

'At that time I had not been in Jersey very long after moving from Madeira,' remembered Portuguese-born Duarte, now the restaurant's head waiter. 'We were very busy that night, but I could tell there was a bad atmosphere, which was strange because I had seen the parents here fairly often with friends and they always seemed to enjoy themselves. I didn't know what they were arguing about, as my English then was not very good, but when I served them it was all very tense.'

Mark, watching several bottles of good wine disappear on top of the substantial earlier intake, made no attempt to hide his disgust at what he considered heavy drinking. Roderick was egging his parents on as if it was an officers' mess booze-up back at his Winchester barracks. His brother looked on with distaste. Worse, Elizabeth's lobster was not the right colour and she was vociferous in her complaints to the head waiter. By midnight she had turned her fire on Roderick, claiming that his plans to abandon his army career after just four years were wrecking her fondest hopes for him.

'I would not say it was a dog fight, but voices were raised and they made us so nervous we forgot to charge them for the lobster. We were not upset when they finally left,' said Duarte.

They left their fellow diners at the restaurant and drove back to the family home, 9 Clos de l'Atlantique in exclusive St Brelade. As Desmond de Silva QC, the ebullient Crown prosecutor, was to tell the packed Gibraltar magistrate's court hearing which was finally to send Roderick back to Jersey six years later: 'That was the last the world was to see of Mr and Mrs Newall.'

At the bungalow, a modest home compared with the Newalls' palatial villa at Javea overlooking the Mediterranean on the Costa Blanca, out came the eighteen-year-old malt whisky and the crystal glasses. But the ill feeling continued, prompting Mark to walk out.

Within the hour, Roderick, trained by the army to

kill, struck. And the weapon which came to hand was a rice flail he grabbed from a box he had cleared earlier from the attic. First he bludgeoned his father Nick over the head as he stood by the fireplace in the lounge. The blows were so violent that blood splattered over the walls, hearth and even the ceiling. The pipe-smoking 56-year-old, who had settled in Jersey for the quiet life of a gentleman of means, died virtually instantly, his skull cracked. There was barely enough time for Elizabeth to flee in horror to the bedroom. Police would never know whether she saw her husband fall or merely heard his dying screams, but they do know that she reached the door to the master bedroom and was trying to slam it as Roderick burst in and battered her to the ground with the rice flail. When he had finished, she lay slumped by the door, blood from the gaping wounds in her head gushing so profusely that it seeped through the deep-pile carpet to the tiles below.

Roderick has always insisted that he was alone in the house, carrying out the killings unaided. In the early hours of that Sunday morning no one heard a sound, despite the fact that a most brutal patricide and matricide had taken place.

The truth was so far beyond belief that senior detectives of the island's CID lost crucial weeks before even accepting this horrific reality . . . and six years before bringing the case to court.

* * *

Roderick gazed at the crumpled bodies of his parents and then, according to the statement he was to make six years later, telephoned brother Mark for help. Mark drove over immediately in a red van – a vehicle which came to play an important part in the long police investigation.

The brothers had hired it from a garage near the island airport the previous afternoon because they claimed they needed to move a mattress from Mark's home back to his previous flat and to collect a bed. Somehow Roderick had contrived to leave his driving licence at home and so he persuaded his father to come with them to sign for the van. As Desmond de Silva was to say in court in Gibraltar, 'Nicholas Newall was in fact to unwittingly hire his own hearse.'

The same day a fair-haired muscular man, speaking in what shop assistant Tina Collins was to describe as a German accent, walked into Jersey's largest builders' merchants. Tina has never forgotten the odd sale: two large tarpaulins, two spades, a pickaxe, a bow saw, six heavy-duty plastic sacks, a length of rope, a box of scalpel knives and two torches. The bill came to £103.42 and the mystery man paid in cash. Was this cold and calculating Roderick buying the tools to murder and bury his parents? Tina could not identify the man. Later, police were to call a major press conference in an effort to trace this man and his tools and sheeting.

Back at the murder scene, the two brothers had to

act quickly. Calculating they had just a few hours until dawn, they swiftly wrapped the plastic sheeting around the bodies. So thorough was their gruesome work that there was still flesh on the bones six years later. With time so pressing they didn't remove even one item of clothing. Elizabeth's Rolex watch, bought in the last De Gruchy spending spree as a birthday present to herself, was still on her wrist. Pathologists who examined the corpse found the Rolex's tiny battery had run down, but the watch was otherwise in perfect working order.

Next, the brothers bound the bodies with the twine so that, as Roderick told his Uncle Stephen years later, 'they were well camouflaged'. Bundling them into the back of the hire van and covering them with the tarpaulin, they sped off through the streets of St Brelade and along the deserted country roads heading north to the playground of their childhood.

Tranquil Grève de Lecq is one of the most beautiful rocky coves and beaches on the holiday island, a leading attraction where tourists walk on the cliffs and laze on the sands. For fourteen years, the brothers had spent their school holidays running, hiding and playing around the woods, stream and the beach beneath the family home perched halfway up the hill and so aptly named the Crow's Nest. Years earlier, in tears, they had buried their pet black labrador, Timmy, in the garden behind the house and marked the grave with a solemn stone so that no one would disturb their best friend.

Now, in those pre-dawn hours, they crept back secretly to bury their slaughtered parents less than a playful scamper away from their pet. This time there were no tears, only the fear of discovery. The bodies were buried, but the cover-up had barely begun.

The first detectives on the case were to spend days investigating the movements of the red van. The only sighting of the van on the open road came from an early riser, who had spotted a similar vehicle being driven south from Grève de Lecq. The brothers were returning to La Falaise, Mark's home. At 6 a.m., Sheila Cruickshank was woken in her next-door house by the sound of car doors slamming in the normally quiet cul-de-sac. The day before, she had noticed Mark's white Toyota MR2 outside his house, along with the red van. Now, as she slipped from her bed and walked down the stairs to a window in the hall, she saw the van with its rear doors open and the Toyota, its boot also open. In the half light she could make out two men passing objects to each other. The brothers were disposing of Roderick's tools of murder and burial and other incriminating evidence. Fifteen minutes later, Mrs Cruickshank heard them driving off, speeding back to the murder scene at 9 Clos de l'Atlantique.

At the bungalow Mark and Roderick set to work with scrubbing brushes, cloths, sponges and kitchen detergents in a desperate effort to scrub the results of Roderick's attack off the walls and carpets. They washed the bloodstained sheets and remade their parents' bed long before the linen was dry. As they worked, a car drew up outside. It was 9 a.m. and their grim work was far from completed. Their unexpected guest was Elizabeth's best friend on the island, Maureen Ellam; she was bearing flowers for Elizabeth's birthday.

Diminutive but feisty, Maureen had known Elizabeth for just a few months, since she and husband David had first wanted to buy the Crow's Nest from them, but her unshakable intuition concerning the fate of Nick and Elizabeth was to prove crucial to the long investigation which followed.

'It was a lovely morning,' she remembers. 'I drove over listening to a church service in French. I am not a house visitor normally, certainly not at that time of the morning, but we knew they had been for a birthday party at the Sea Crest with the boys and they planned to leave the island in a few days' time to drive back to their other home in Spain.

'Someone had given me a large bouquet of flowers, because it was my birthday then as well. There were so many I didn't know what to do with them, so I thought: "What a lovely idea to give some to Elizabeth."

'I took over a plant she had picked from our greenhouse for a friend and also Nick's mosquito killer, which he had lent to me but wanted to take back to Spain.

10

'"Ah," I thought, "these are my visiting cards," but I didn't plan on seeing them. Elizabeth would still be in bed or, more likely, soaking in the bath with a cup of coffee. Nick would be out picking up the newspapers.

'So when I pulled up outside the house and saw a strange car, a white Toyota, I realized Roderick must be staying with them. There was no way the Roderick I knew would have stayed at Mark's house. I didn't expect him to be up; he is a youngster and always unconscious at that time of the day.

'I rang the bell anyway, put the flowers on the doorstep and ran back to collect the plant and the spray from the car, never expecting anyone to open the door, but there, very quickly, stood Roderick, red-faced and dishevelled. He was dressed in a red V-neck pullover and jumper and fawn corduroy trousers. "My, the young up before the old," I said to him. I picked up the plant and spray from the car and walked towards him. He answered very quickly – too quickly – "Yes, they are still asleep."

'I said, "Christ, that was some night, wasn't it?" Roderick looked stoned out of his mind, like a chap with a hangover. I felt something horrific, it is called vibes, which you cannot explain to the police. What I do recall was that his face was scarlet; he looked like a man in a daze. I thought again: "Wow, what a night."

'I said, "Still asleep?" It was unbelievable. Nick would not have been asleep, of that I was certain. He

11

was always an early riser regardless of what time he had been to bed.

'Picking up the flowers I said to him, "Here you are, lay them on the bed, and when your mother opens her eyes she will think she has died."

'We chatted on about other things. I said to Roderick that I was still waiting for him to come over and see what we had done to his old home, as his mother had said he would be interested. But he just stood there staring, so much so that I said to him, "You know who I am, don't you?" He was so switched off, he shook his head and apologized. I said, "The Crow's Nest," and he replied, "Yes, of course."

'I now know he was waiting all the time for me to say something, wanting to know, asking himself had I seen anything in the early hours of that morning. He must have heard from his parents that I am a person who does not sleep. I could well have been looking out from the terrace up the valley. Yes, that was certainly true, but I did not recall anything. If I had glimpsed any movement I would have dismissed it as a courting couple.

'Anyway, at such times I like to look the other way, out to sea, to the lights of the fishing boats, the marker buoys and the coast of France; there is always activity out there.

'But he was very worried . . .'

Maureen turned and drove off, but already doubts were starting to dominate her thoughts, long before

12

church-going islanders were thinking of morning service or autumn holidaymakers considering a walk at Grève de Lecq.

'Nick would certainly not be asleep,' she mused. 'Then I thought, "Oh well, Roderick is just trying to stop me marching into the bedroom and disturbing them."'

Later, she found out that Mark had been in the house as well. 'I can imagine the two of them had seen me driving up. The venetian blinds were closed, but you could see looking out from the inside. I bet they said, "Gawd, look who it is!"

'You see, Mark would have shuddered at seeing me at such a time and told Roderick: "You answer the door and get rid of her."

'When I got home, I fully expected Elizabeth would have called to say thank you for the flowers. When David said nobody had rung, I thought, "That's bloody funny, what's wrong?"'

If Roderick and Mark thought they had got rid of Maureen Ellam, they were very wrong. They had just aroused the suspicions of the one woman on the island capable of starting Jersey's biggest manhunt and keeping it going, earning herself the nickname of 'Miss Marple' in the process.

2

Missing Persons – the Cover-up

As Maureen Ellam prepared Sunday lunch, still turning over in her mind the strange events of the morning caused by her doorstep confrontation with Roderick, she waited for the phone call from Elizabeth.

'In the end I decided not to call her and check up because at the end of the day you cannot phone someone, no matter how close, to say: "You haven't phoned to thank me for the flowers,"' she explained. 'I knew she had got them because I had taken them to the house. Now I regret not picking up the phone.'

Roderick and Mark were not content with their clean-up operation at the bungalow until 10 a.m. By this time the carpets were soaked and the walls dripping with detergents and water. Before they left, they turned up the central heating to maximum and closed all the windows and doors.

They loaded the red van with all the cleaning materials, including blood-soaked kitchen towels and rags, and drove to La Falaise, Mark's home, in the next stage of the cover-up. They knocked on the door of Mark's neighbours, Maureen and Daniel Bickerton, asking if they could burn rubbish legally on nearby Noirmont Common. The Bickertons were surprised by the call, but they were certain it was at 2 p.m. because almost at the same time they had received a phone call from Daniel's mother in Newcastle and then Maureen had had to go and visit her mother in hospital at 2.30 p.m.

This was another blunder which was to throw doubt on the brothers' cover story. For, a few days later, they were to insist to police that at that precise time they were having a farewell lunch with their parents. An hour later, they hurriedly dumped the mattress at Mark's old house opposite a B&Q Superstore in the village of St John. Tracy Le Nevue, who had shared the running costs of the house with Mark, was one of his former work colleagues in St Helier and, ironically, a policewoman. She was surprised to see him on the doorstep. They had not bothered to phone to say they were coming. In great haste they shifted the mattress in and took a bed away. Refusing an offer of coffee, they told her they were in a hurry to catch flights back to the mainland.

But sometime that day, before they drove to the airport, they had a far more important task than delivering mattresses. And again they chose familiar childhood territory: the woods above the Crow's Nest

16

at La Vallette. There they set fire to the final evidence of murder. This included their father's glasses which, they knew, he would never have left home without.

The brothers caught separate flights to Gatwick, but before they left the island the red van was returned to the hire company in a very clean condition. The inside had been scrubbed and hosed down. As their aircraft lifted off from Jersey's short runway, they prepared to return to their respectable lives and to wait for tearful phone calls informing them that their parents were missing.

That night, Angela Barnes, Nicholas and Elizabeth's close friend on the island for twenty-six years, phoned their house and was disappointed to get no reply. A wealthy widow in her late sixties, she knew many of the Newall family and it was her determination in keeping contact with relatives and also the police over the years of the investigation that was to help tighten the noose around Roderick's neck and net Mark as his accomplice.

As the days ticked by friends grew more and more concerned, yet it was not until the eighth day that police were alerted to the fact that Nicholas and Elizabeth were missing.

It was clearly out of character for the gushy Elizabeth – who spent so much time on the telephone that she was known as 'The Great Communicator' – not to have made contact with anyone in all that time. Nor did she ever miss appointments. Yet on Monday, just two days after that last supper, she failed to turn up at Hettich, a leading Jersey jewellers, to collect an exclusive watch she had ordered. The next day she failed to show for a game of badminton with Mary Lamey at a local sports club and missed a dinner date with other island friends.

No one could get a reply from the Newalls' phone to find out why. This went on all week. The couple failed to keep dentist and doctor appointments, the postman got no reply and, most importantly, they did not show up for a long-planned visit to Uncle Kenneth, the diminutive invalid who lived on the nearby tiny island of Sark. Yet no one dialled the police emergency number. Looking back, the friends all agree they could not come to terms with their growing apprehension that something dreadful had happened to the happy couple.

Meanwhile Mark had sneaked back to Jersey unnoticed. Five days after he had helped to wrap the bodies of his mother and father in plastic sheeting and bury them, he took the evening flight from Heathrow and collected his car from the island's airport car park. In less than an hour he had driven to his home, La Falaise, then to his former office to collect tickets and documents, and on to the harbour to catch the night ferry to Portsmouth. He had made sure that none of his parents' friends knew that he was briefly back on the island. Next morning, he drove from Portsmouth to Winchester for a crisis meeting with Roderick at the Sir John Moore Barracks, headquarters of the Royal Green Jackets, to assess how well the cover-up was going.

After lunch with Roderick, a lieutenant in the fashionable regiment, and fellow officer Mark Manghan, he drove back to London. He and Roderick could well be content. There was still no sign of an alarm.

But bells were ringing at the Crow's Nest. 'Thursday 15 October was Elizabeth's birthday. I knew she was going to be at home regardless of where she and Nick had buggered off to those last few days,' said Maureen Ellam. 'So that morning I telephone every half an hour. I had a birthday card which played "Happy Birthday to You" which I had ready to play as soon as I heard her voice.' Dialling and redialling, Maureen's frustration and anxiety grew. 'Where the four and half is she?' she wondered.

It had been windy the previous night and the great storm which was to devastate the island and much of southern England was about to strike. 'We were expecting them round for dinner on the Friday, and as we cleaned up after the hurricane, I could not stop thinking what the hell might have happened to them. I managed to get hold of Mark's telephone number at La Falaise, although it was ex-directory. But when I rang there was just an answer phone. I expected that. In his mind he is rather too important to answer the telephone.'

So the dinner party for the Newalls came and went. The phone remained silent and there were two empty chairs at the table. By Saturday morning, Maureen, in her word, was 'psychotic'. She decided the time had come to act.

Robert Shearer and his friend Christopher Poirrier had just finished breakfast at their home next door to 9 Clos de l'Atlantique and were preparing for work at the airport when the phone rang. Maureen Ellam had taken the first step along the route to the truth. Shearer and Poirrier told her they had not seen the Newalls for several days, although Nick's metallic grey Citroën was parked outside. Urged on by Maureen, Shearer agreed to check the house, and he rang the doorbell several times and checked the windows. Under further pressure from Maureen, he then climbed over the wall into the Newalls' back garden. Picking his way between the storm-damaged trees and shattered greenhouse, he was able to open the rear patio door, which was unlocked. As he entered the house, calling out 'Anyone in?' he was struck by the heat. It was like an oven. The central heating control had been overridden and the thermostat was on maximum. Robert Shearer's discovery of a deserted house, the baking heat and spotless kitchen at last triggered a response.

Maureen now knew for certain that something was very wrong and she sent her husband David in the family car to investigate. He managed to get past the fallen trees that blocked the roads, walking the last mile to reach the Newalls' place. The first thing he noticed was Nick's car keys on the kitchen table, where he had left them when he returned from the last supper almost a week previously. David Ellam checked the telephone was working normally and then called Mark in London, leaving an urgent message. He thought that the house looked unusually tidy. This surprised him, because Elizabeth was a notoriously untidy person.

At 12.30 p.m. the phone rang at the Crow's Nest. 'Mark, hello love, a bit of a problem. Got any idea of the whereabouts of your parents?' said Maureen, trying to conceal her fears.

'Well, no,' he replied in his precise way. She told him that her husband was at that moment at the Newall home because no one had seen Nick and Elizabeth since the previous weekend. This, said Maureen, was out of character.

'Yes it is, Mrs Ellam,' came the same straight-faced reply. Mark was always formal with the Ellams. But he added with a slight edge, 'Is he there now?'

Over the next twenty-four hours she and Mark broke the news to the rest of the family in the island, London, Scotland and Spain. The police at their headquarters in St Helier were also given the information, and the duty woman police constable told Maureen to fill out a missing persons report.

On Sunday, Roderick flew to Jersey, to be met by Maureen and David, who took him straight to the house. 'He sat in the back, every inch the soldier. I told him to hang on to his air ticket because "We will charge the buggers when they turn up." "Too right," he replied,' recalled Maureen.

'As we drove we were all very friendly. When we reached the house Roderick was out like a shot. Normally no one is quicker than me in getting out of a car and into a house. But this time he was in the side door before I had got the seat belt off.'

Once in the murder house, watching Roderick prowling from room to room without saying a word, she felt that something was wrong. Roderick appeared confused. He was searching the house, checking in the fridge and wardrobes. Maureen noticed the flowers she had given the boy to pass on to his mother the previous week. They were dead in a vase on top of the sideboard.

Maureen was as surprised as her husband, given Elizabeth's untidiness, that everything was clean and tidy. Followed closely by Roderick, she went into the master bedroom to continue her investigation. Spotting what she thought was a coffee stain by the door, she bent down and noticed that the carpet had been pulled back and replaced, using nails. She had stumbled across the exact spot where her best friend had died in a pool of her own blood, which the boys had vainly tried to mop up.

'More than the stain, I could see the pattern of the fluffed-up carpet. That's what gave the game away and again I was uneasy. But it never occurred to me that it was blood. It was coffee: about the size of a cupful.' But there were more tell-tale signs: 'The bed was made; it was a duvet. Elizabeth never made the bed until she was ready to get into it. It looked wrong. I said to David, quite loud so that Roderick could hear, "These sheets have been washed but not ironed, and what's more nobody has slept in them." They were not damp, they were hard; I could smell soap powder. If you run an iron over bed linen it softens it, and if you sleep in new linen for just one night it removes that lovely smell of fresh laundry.

'One policeman was to ask me if I thought that the bed could have been made up with damp sheets. I replied, "That is exactly what has happened. That bed had not been slept in."'

The Ellams drove straight to police headquarters at Rouge Bouillon in St Helier, followed by Roderick at the wheel of his father's car – the aroma of the dead man's ever-present pipe tobacco in his nostrils.

For WPC Sarah Martin it was to be the most extraordinary report she had ever handled. At 4.40 p.m. that Sunday afternoon, a handsome young officer marched up to her enquiry desk to report his parents missing, his nerves in the family house now replaced with bravado. Asked how he would describe his missing mother, Roderick considered his answer, gazing towards the ceiling. 'Jolly hockey sticks,' he replied. Maureen Ellam, sitting at a desk to write her report, was shocked. 'Roderick, you sound just like your father,' she scolded, surprised at a side of a boy that she had not witnessed before. It made little difference. Asked how he would describe his mother's voice, the public-school-educated and Sandhurst-trained Roderick arrogantly sneered back, 'Give me a few adjectives to choose from.'

'Roderick, come off it, you are going too far now,' Maureen snapped, shocked at this attitude towards a young policewoman trying to do her job in difficult circumstances. What surprised Maureen was Roderick's flippant attitude, considering that his parents were missing and that something terrible might have happened to them.

'All this time he appeared to have no concern for his parents. There was a coldness about him. Maybe being British, with a stiff upper lip and all that, might have a lot to do with it. The parents did their own thing and the boys always had to cope for themselves.

'For example, there was a big outcry on the island when it became known that Mark had taken the Sunday-afternoon flight out and then returned on Tuesday to pick up his car, and taken the ferry back the same night without bothering to contact his parents. We know now that he knew they were dead. But even if they had been alive and well he would not have bothered to pick up the phone or call round.'

Roderick declined supper at the Ellams' and drove his father's car out of the police car park.

The following day Maureen received two telling phone calls. 'Roderick was all uptight. He said the police were not interested in his missing parents. All they wanted to know was what he and his brother had been doing. His voice was high, almost screeching, at me; he was on a high.' Then Angela Barnes rang. 'Do you know Roderick slept in his parents' bed last night?' she asked in a horrified tone. Maureen's pulse quickened. Why did he do that? There were two other beds made up. He had slept in that bed to get rid of the smell of clean linen. How could he have done that? Did he get a kick from it, a high, a dare? 'He had heard me say that the bed had not been slept in and he must have thought he would put that right and so destroy the evidence. But what he must have been thinking as he got into the bed I just cannot imagine.'

Jim Adamson parked his black Ford Fiesta XR2 car in the reserved area of Rouge Bouillon Police Headquarters that Monday after a long weekend off. It was quiet, so he went down for a chat and a cup of tea with the duty sergeant, Alan Alchin. It was 10 a.m. on Monday 19 October 1987, and it was the first time he was to hear the name Newall. It was a missing persons case.

The Scottish detective sergeant, then aged 37, checked the missing persons report filed the previous day, noticed that the Newalls were due to be in Spain for that week, phoned their villa over his second cup of tea and, getting no reply, wondered aloud whether they had been caught up in the great storm.

He called over to a colleague to let him know when the Newalls' sons came in. They arrived just after 1 p.m. accompanied by Maureen Ellam. Adamson took them across to the CID interview room, where their elaborate and much-rehearsed cover-up story was unfolded for the first time.

After the champagne and candlelit birthday dinner at the Sea Crest they had returned to Clos de l'Atlantique for a drink before returning to Mark's house for the night. The following morning they had returned to their parents' home for breakfast, stayed for lunch washed down by two bottles of white wine, then left them in good health to catch their afternoon flights back to the UK.

They said that their parents often went for long walks, particularly around nearby sand dunes. Something might have happened to them while they were out rambling. They also said they were concerned that their parents could have been caught in the storm, that they could have both been blown over a cliff.

After this first meeting, some detectives were convinced the Newalls' disappearance was sinister and that their sons knew more than they were admitting.

Later that afternoon, Detective Inspector Graham Nimmo and Adamson searched the house with Roderick and Mark. They found the empty champagne bottles, drunk at the start of the birthday dinner party nine days before, on the utility room floor, but there was no sign of the empty wine bottles from the Sunday lunch. In the lounge was the malt whisky, with three glasses on the coffee table left over from the party. In the spare bedroom all the Newalls' luggage was ready for them to take to their villa in Spain.

The detectives' suspicions were to be aroused again when they took Mark aside for a quiet word. Roderick kept interrupting and had to be told to wait outside.

That evening, four of Jersey's senior CID officers met and decided to step up the investigation, opening an incident room at police headquarters.

The following day, a pale-looking Mark was interviewed at the Atlantic Hotel, one of Jersey's finest, underlining his up-market lifestyle. He picked his words carefully in answering every question. He explained that when Maureen Ellam had called with the birthday flowers the morning after the party, he had hidden in the lounge of his parents' house to keep out of the way. He had let Roderick do the talking because he did not want to speak to Maureen.

It was now two weeks since the Newalls had been last seen. The house and the surrounding area had been examined, their favourite walks searched, friends and relatives interviewed, but no one had any clues as to their whereabouts. The whole island was on alert; missing person posters, with photographs of the Newalls' faces, television and radio appeals all failed to turn up the slightest clue.

Mark returned to the City, Roderick to his regiment. Both sensed that detectives had very serious doubts about their stories, but so far their cover-up appeared to be watertight.

3

'Something Illogical Has Happened'

With police suspicions clearly roused and rumours running wild around the island, Mark decided to counter with his own PR, giving interviews to both the press and television in Jersey. He gave a cool, at times even a cold, performance. Instead of displaying a distraught, tearful reaction to a heart-breaking mystery, Mark said he was seeking a rational or logical explanation of what had happened to his parents.

'If you look at the available facts in a logical way, they do not fit any of the theories of an accident, kidnap, suicide or murder, and therefore the odds are that something illogical has happened to them,' he told the *Jersey Evening Post*. 'Either way it just does not make any sense.'

It was as if he was talking in a City wine bar with his yuppie chums about a failed business deal or the latest rumour in the stockmarket. Dressed in his normal business attire, the fringe of the 21-year-old's blow-dried hair occasionally fell across gold-rimmed glasses, but never disguised his haughty and at times uninterested expression.

'If you are to look at it realistically, then the chances of them being alive are very slim,' he added with a sniff. 'People just don't disappear and then walk through the door three weeks later and say "Hi folks".'

Mark went through the account he had given the police. 'Others are a lot surer about their clothing than I am. By the time we left the house on Sunday my parents were certainly wearing casual clothes – I know what sort of clothing they would have been wearing but I cannot be certain exactly what.'

Asked if his parents had any enemies or business problems in Spain, he replied, 'I know very little about Spain and their life there. But had there been any problem, I would have been the first to know, particularly if it was financial.'

His performance cut no ice with the police, who had already formed a number of questions for the brothers. In a cupboard in the bungalow, detectives discovered rat poison. Had this been used to spike the drinks? They had also found two empty champagne bottles, drunk before the Sea Crest dinner, but no trace of the two wine bottles from which Mark said they had drunk at the Sunday lunch with their parents. This was puzzling.

Had this meal ever taken place? Roderick and Mark's accounts of the Sunday lunch, detailing who sat where and what they ate, did not match.

Mark was staying at the plush Atlantic Hotel, with its sauna, jacuzzi, heated swimming pool and sports complex, rather than at his own home La Falaise. Why?

Two weeks after the disappearance police were no nearer to answering these questions satisfactorily.

Elizabeth's sister Nan, and her husband Dr Alistair Clark, a police surgeon, had rushed back from their own villa in Spain after hearing of the disappearance and had told police that a motorcruiser Nick had once owned had been involved in drug running.

Nan said that Nick had sold the boat, called *September Tide*, to a Dutchman who had turned up at Javea with a suitcase full of guilders. The sale, she said, had been arranged through London-based brokers Camper and Nicholson, and a few months later the Dutchman and three others had been arrested on the boat in Belgium with a large haul of hashish.

Suggestions of drug running were to resurface regularly throughout the investigation, with fingers pointing at various times at both Nicholas and Roderick. Spain is a well-known channel into northern Europe for hashish, the Newall villa was on a Costa renowned as a haven for British criminals on the run, and both had made many trips to and from Jersey. But in the six-year investigation, no concrete evidence of a drug connection ever came to light.

Investigating officers Graham Nimmo and Jim Adamson decided to go to Javea to check on the Newalls' Spanish way of life, while leading forensic scientist David Northcott was called in from the Home Office Laboratories at Aldermaston to examine the bungalow. It took two days for the officers to reach the Spanish town, but only another two days to get themselves arrested.

They travelled by ferry to Portsmouth, and by bus to London before flying to Alicante, where they hired a car and drove to Javea. There, they found a luxury Spanish villa in the hills overlooking the Mediterranean. Persian rugs decorated whitewashed walls and lush green lawns surrounded the swimming pool. But the officers, accompanied by Nan Clark, found nothing obviously germane to their investigation.

After a day interviewing friends and neighbours among the wealthy ex-pat community living in the tax-free haven, they received a message from Interpol ordering them to visit the Spanish police. Next morning, to record this moment of co-operation, Adamson took a photograph of Nimmo outside the local police station.

'Next thing, Graham and I were arrested by armed police for taking a photograph of their headquarters. They kept us for about an hour and were not interested that we were police officers investigating a potentially serious crime,' said Adamson. 'Eventually the captain threw us out and we went for a coffee with a tipple in it. We were ready for that, as we believed we would never get out. We decided not to go near the police again. However, it turned out that we should have gone to the National Police and not the Civil Guard, which is the paramilitary force.'

Back in Jersey there had been progress. Northcott had found blood – lots of it.

David Northcott is renowned as one of the most experienced and able scientists available for police work. He has been called in for some for the most difficult and delicate enquiries in Britain over the last twenty years.

One of the most important was the Devil's Dyke child sex attack in Brighton in 1990. Local police had arrested Russell Bishop four years earlier for a double child murder known as the 'Babes in the Wood' case, but he was cleared in a sensational trial after the forensic evidence and police work had been discredited.

When police arrested Bishop again for the Devil's Dyke attack, in which a little girl was abducted and left for dead at the beauty spot on the Sussex Downs after being brutally abused, the case caused as much of an outcry in Brighton as the Newall case was to do in Jersey. This time, the police had to get it right, and Northcott's evidence, which pinned the crime down to just one man in hundreds of thousands, was vital in Bishop being sentenced to life imprisonment.

Now Northcott, the precise and dapper civil-service scientist with the trademark heavyweight briefcase of his profession, confirmed the fears of every senior officer in Jersey: the Newalls had been violently murdered in their own home. Desmond de Silva was to sum up the results of Northcott's investigation when he told the extradition hearing in Gibraltar six years later, 'It is the case of the Crown that they were done to death in their own home that night.' In their frantic clean-up operation the brothers had missed the fine spray of blood that had landed on dark surfaces.

Said Mr de Silva, 'On October 10 the maid, Netti, had cleaned the glass of a picture above the fireplace in the lounge, first with a damp cloth, then a dry one. Mr Northcott was later to find spots of blood across the picture. From the distribution of the blood splattering which had missed the eyes of whosoever cleaned up blood from the floor level to the ceiling, he concluded that someone had suffered a violent attack in that room.'

The scientist also stated in his report that blood had soaked through the carpet and underlay in front of the fire. 'At some stage someone was lying on the carpet long enough to lose a large quantity of blood,' he wrote.

That 'someone' could only have been Nicholas Newall. Blood in the bedroom also pointed to the fact that Elizabeth had been killed just inside the door of the master bedroom – without a shadow of doubt, two scenes of violence, two scenes of murder.

The expert found that the fireside rug was missing. It was so bloodstained that the brothers, police were certain, had had to remove it.

Later, Professor James 'Taffy' Cameron, a Home Office pathologist who gave evidence in the 'Dingo Baby' trial in Australia, and was in the island helping Dr Northcott, concluded that the attacks had been carried out with a blunt instrument. Dr Northcott showed detectives where he had traced the bloodmarks. They ran the whole length of the wall to the ceiling in the lounge and stained the carpet, wall and mirror. There was also a bloodstained footprint on the lounge door.

These findings were a breakthrough, but why had Jersey scene-of-crime officers missed these marks after two detectives had found a bloodspot on a poker in the fireplace? Vital weeks had been lost before David Northcott was eventually called in.

According to Nan Clark, it was Nimmo and Adamson who found the bloodspot and one of the detectives agreed that mistakes had been made: 'It was thought at first that the spot was too bright to be blood, but we had it analysed and that is what it turned out to be. In fact, it was about the biggest spot discovered in the whole house,' he said. 'It is hard to say if there was an oversight, that stains had been missed. It might have been a lack of experience, I suppose. But a few people were thinking at the time that the Newalls were still alive, possibly in Spain.'

With Northcott's findings, no one was now in any doubt that this was a murder hunt. And Roderick and Mark Newall were the prime suspects.

4

The Newall Nut

The fortune which created the envy, hate and greed that caused the Newall clan to split itself apart was built on the 'Newall Nut'.

Roderick's grandfather, Archibald Newall, founded the family business on an industrial complex near the centre of Glasgow between the two world wars. He supplied the shipbuilding industry, on which the empire depended, with nuts and bolts. At that time the 'Newall Nut' was a well-known basic component for yards along the Clyde; it even had its own peculiar thread. After the Second World War, the nuts and bolts were supplied to the old Albion Motor Works which specialized in lorries before it was taken over by British Leyland.

Archibald's wife gave birth to twins in 1931, but they were very different characters. Nicholas was never burdened by his father's work ethic, while Stephen remained in Scotland to continue the family engineering tradition. Stephen still has his own factory in Rhu in Strathclyde, overlooking the Gare Loch. His roots are firmly embedded in Scotland: the family home is a gaunt granite building at Rhu, his weekend retreat is the tiny island of Shauna in Loch Linnie, also on the west coast. The private island is shared with a shepherd, his flock and a few cattle, power is supplied by a generator, the few guests he welcomes are ferried across the loch in an open boat called *The Pig*, followed by a drive in a pick-up truck along a dirt track.

Stephen coveted his privacy and was proud of keeping the family name respected in Scotland. Twin brother Nicholas did not care about tradition; as one friend said on Jersey, 'I don't think he accomplished one single thing in his entire life.'

And then there was Kenneth. Archibald's brother was equally wealthy, but chose to live on the island of Sark. He was barely four foot six inches tall and became almost a recluse, agonizing over who was to inherit his £1 million estate. It was in Sark that the clan gathered just one month before Nick and Elizabeth were murdered to pressurize the little man into altering his will so that its proceeds should be shared between his identical twin nephews Stephen and Nicholas. *Their* children would then inherit their share in turn.

One family friend was to tell the high society magazine, *Tatler*, on the fifth anniversary of the murders: 'Kenneth was one of the most bizarre factors in the case. He was a tiny, fat fellow with a big round face and you honestly could not tell what sex he was. He had incredibly long fingernails and you could see what he had been eating for the last three days from the front of his shirt.'

Always a generous, if lonely man, he died heartbroken in November 1987 a few weeks after Nick and Elizabeth failed to turn up for their regular visit and he was told they had been murdered and that there was no trace of their bodies. Again the clan was summoned to attend his funeral in Guernsey. Inevitably, the occasion was marred by a family row over the unsolved mystery.

In the late 1950s, Nicholas, rather than bother himself with engineering, had taken himself off to St Andrews University with the vague idea of a career in education. During his studies he met Elizabeth, a fellow student, and later they married and set up home in Motherwell. They had two sons, Roderick Innes Nelson born in Glasgow in 1965, and Mark Stephen Nelson born a year later in St Andrews. While Stephen toiled through the hard economic climate of the mid-1960s Nicholas decided to take his wife, his sons and a Scottish nanny to a new life in the sunshine of the Caribbean, where fortunes went a lot further. Nick and Elizabeth were keen sailors, and in 1967 they left home for the last time to set sail for the West Indies, leaving behind his mundane job as a schoolteacher.

En route they pulled into the island of Jersey where, twenty years later, they were to be battered to death by one of these babes in arms. After loading supplies for the cross-Atlantic haul, they set sail again. But only a day out from Jersey the nanny became ill and the family returned to the island. Their Caribbean dream having faded, Nick and Elizabeth waited for the nanny to recover and, to their surprise, found themselves falling in love with the island. They set up their first home in Jersey at Martello Lodge in St Brelade's Bay.

As teaching was the only job he knew, Nicholas took up part-time work, drumming history into the offspring of the rich at prep schools. In his oceans of spare time he sat at home, smoking his pipe and writing books and plays. These included a novel called *The Dawlish Twins*, another about a prep-school teacher, a murder mystery and a play about the execution of Mary Queen of Scots, which he called *The Honest Man*.

These manuscripts were found gathering dust in his house after his death. Despite countless letters, he never found a publisher. It was one of the bitterest disappointments in the life of a man who prided himself on his love of the arts. One acquaintance suggested later that Nick's pretensions regarding literature were symptoms of a rebellion against a cantankerous father's obsessions with machinery, production lines and grime.

While Nick had his nose in his books, the exuberant Elizabeth was down at the sports clubs playing tennis and badminton, establishing her face in Jersey society. The boys were looked after by a nanny before being packed off to the best prep school on the island, St Michael's. The only times they came to Nick's notice were the odd occasions they attended his history lessons.

The Newalls' love of yachts was never impeded by their young family. Roderick, who was to become an expert yachtsman, got his taste for the sea aboard one of his parents' first boats, the *Banana Blush*. *September Tide*, a fifty-four-foot twin-screw diesel yacht, was to follow – their pride and joy, as it was built by J. Silver at the Roseneath yard, close to their old Scottish home. After it was sold in February 1975 for £13,000, the next yacht to be tied up at the Newalls' berth in one of Jersey's top marinas was *Chanson de Lecq*, named after the beloved cove below the Crow's Nest on the northwest coast of the island.

The Mediterranean sun was their next target. Spending their inheritance was never a problem for Nick and Elizabeth; the thought of making provision for the future never crossed their minds. In 1977 they bought a dream villa in El Trencal, near Javea, a tranquil fishing port close to Alicante on Spain's Costa Blanca – the white coast. It bore many similarities to the Crow's Nest, set in the hills overlooking the old Spanish town with a sweeping panorama of the Costa beaches and the Mediterranean. For Elizabeth, it was straight into the exclusive El Trancal Tennis Club and the Javea Yacht Club, where their current yacht was moored.

They were to spend a great deal of time at their Spanish hacienda, with its swimming pool, socializing with the wealthy ex-pat Britons in a non-stop round of sundowners, sangria and barbecues in the warm Spanish nights.

Nick had even less of an appetite for finance than he did for his father's business. He was a Lloyd's name, and in those days this meant a no-risk, big return investment which helped pay for the lavish lifestyle. In the mid-1980s he turned responsibility for all his assets and investments over to Mark, then still in his teens and barely out of public school.

Mark had started his financial career as a trainee broker at Barclaytrust in St Helier before moving to Sheppards, the Jersey branch of a major finance house. But there was a time bomb ticking away in the portfolio. A major proportion of Nicholas's investments were in a Lloyd's syndicate headed by Richard Outhwaite; distinguished fellow names were Edward Heath, Rocco Forte and sport stars Tony Jacklin and Virginia Wade. Nicholas's syndicate took on heavy asbestos risks, shortly before the £2 billion asbestosis disaster swept the insurance world. A total of £260 million was lost. A close friend has said that Nick would have been penniless had he been alive today.

Mark was astute enough to see the danger coming and in a series of bitter rows begged his father to get out. The peril of Mark's future inheritance was all too clear. As he told the local island newspaper in that cold interview given within days of burying his parents in their secret grave, he would have known of any problems and business connections that could be linked to the mystery.

This was not the only concern young Mark had about his dad's shaky financial dealings: there was a bad deal in Lanzarote in the Canary Islands. Nick and others had ploughed large sums of money into land which turned out to be useless because there was no planning permission.

All the time Nick had little contact with his own shrewd brother Stephen. Only a few times did he and Elizabeth make the long journey up to Scotland. His branch of the family were effectively cut off, as the clan drifted apart.

Although the investments were in place and assets fixed, day-to-day spending money sometimes reached a hand-to-mouth basis. A year before Roderick was to bludgeon them to death a neighbour described them as 'looking bloody hard-up'. He added, 'They had an old Peugeot to drive back and forward to Spain. It was the sort of car that you feared a wheel might fall off when you opened the door.'

But there was always something to keep them ticking over, even if it was selling their main asset, the

Crow's Nest, in September 1986. They made £200,000 profit on the sale, so after buying the modest bungalow in Clos de l'Atlantique for £82,000 and paying his debts, Nick was £100,000 in the black.

5

The Brothers

Nicholas Newall did not want children and, despite being a prep-school teacher, never liked them. Ever since Roderick and Mark had been born, he had dismissed them to their faces as 'Elizabeth's boys'.

Roderick's only explanation of why he hated his parents so much came in a tearful confession to girlfriend Helena Pedo: 'Because they packed me off to school when I was three.'

At St Michael's there was certainly no favouritism shown by Nicholas to the boys; in fact he had trouble recognizing them. Teachers at the school can still recall an astonishing episode which aptly summed up his attitude to his children. Roderick, then aged eight, was excelling at sport and was confident of dominating sports day. He was thrilled to find out that his father had turned up with a cine camera, then an expensive toy for the rich, to film his certain triumph. Nicholas's camera did indeed record a small blond boy breaking the tape in a great victory, but to Roderick's shame and humiliation, his father had mistakenly filmed the wrong boy in the wrong race. With no hint of an apology or even embarrassment, Nicholas gave the film to the other boy's parents with a dismissive shrug.

They received first-class education at the best schools, but the boys' lives were devoid of love. Maureen Ellam, the family's astute friend, says now, 'They were four very different people, four very volatile people. Nick and Mark silently seethed with anger at each other, Elizabeth and Roderick were two shouters and bawlers. There were clashes all the time over everything; it was unbelievable, at times so awful it was funny. It all started at their earliest schooldays – I don't think the boys had a kiss or a cuddle from their parents all their lives.'

The boys' happiest times were spent away from their parents. In school holidays, while their parents were in Spain, it was left to Nan Clark, their aunt in London, to play the surrogate mother, and Uncle Stephen allowed Roderick, right up to his army days, to have the run of his island home and to bring friends there. But all the time Mark was withdrawing deeper into himself, building up the arrogant front which he knew so annoyed his father.

Said Maureen, 'I knew they had the support of the aunts and uncles and, despite the absence of their parents around them, they really had every privilege that life can offer: good educations, they were taught to sail, to snorkel, to water-ski; whatever they wanted they had. They had great freedom here in Jersey; as small children they ran wild over the fields, in the woods and on the beach . . .'

From St Michael's in Jersey they passed on through the rich people's education mill to Lockers Park School in Hertfordshire and then on the Radley College, Oxfordshire, one of Britain's finest public schools, where the Princess of Wales considered sending her two sons.

There is an old adage that the only thing Etonians and Harrovians can agree on is the fact that they all hate Radleians. In such company one contemporary of the Newall boys, who now does 'something in the City', described Mark as 'a shit among shits'. Even in the context of Britain's often bizarre public-school traditions, Radley is considered peculiar. The headmaster is called the warden, teachers are called dons and the houses are called socials. The school's motto is 'Sicut serpentes, sicut columbae' ('As wise as serpents, as gentle as doves'). Today its 600 pupils pay more than £11,000 a year for the privilege of attending. Its massive playing fields constitute the largest mown area in Europe and the school still maintains a beagle pack which hunts twice a year.

When Roderick and Mark arrived as awestruck 13-year-old new boys at the 146-year-old school, the then headmaster Dennis Silk solemnly addressed them in the chapel, as he did every new arrival. With a sweep of the hand gesturing to the stained-glass windows, he told them, 'We regard this side of what we do here as the most important side of all. You will spend a small part of each day in here, but the real religious life begins when you walk out of the door.

'Some of you may be blessed with good brains, others not. That does not matter twopence; it is how hard you try . . . you come to school for one thing – to acquire the right habits for life.'

Whatever habits Roderick and Mark acquired at Radley certainly did not include brotherly love. In a virtually unprecedented move, masters had to place the brothers in separate houses and even send them home on different trains because of the incessant rows they feared would escalate into violence.

Anthony Hudson, now headmaster of Pangbourne School, was in charge of Roderick's house, 'F' social. The tall, dark-haired, imposing history don is very much the establishment type and is extremely guarded in recalling any memories of the boy. He regards the housemaster's relationship with his boys as a privileged position. 'It is not the confessional but it is not right I should reveal what went on, although I might be naïve about that,' he says now. However, he does disclose, in his extremely understated style, that Roderick was 'disappointed' by the lack of love and support from his parents, who despite the great distance visited Radley once a term, parking their camper van overnight at the bottom of the school grounds. This well-meaning gesture merely heaped further humiliation and mortification on the boys, who were ridiculed for this 'common and vulgar' action of their parents.

'They would come, watch Roderick if he was playing sport, go to the chapel and speak to me at length. It would be unfair to say they totally ignored the boy,' said Mr Hudson. But he did detect 'an atmosphere' between Roderick and his parents and, typically careful not not point the finger directly, added most revealingly, 'To get the best out of school and enjoy it there has to be teamwork between parents, teachers and boy together. Maybe Roderick did not have the full teamwork.'

'F' social was always the house for the elitist boys – the best rugby players, the best athletes, the best music scholars – and Roderick never quite made it, according to school friends. 'He was always on the fringe of everything and never quite got accepted. He wanted to be part of the rugby gang, and was a bit of a hard nut on the field, but he was never a good enough sportsman, although he would have liked to have been,' said one. 'He was bright but not the brightest. He was in Shell 2, the semi-fast stream, but he was never considered for Oxford. Chemistry was his strong point and, being a bit of a loner, he would spend hours by himself mucking about with bits of equipment . . . '

Roderick was desperate for acceptance and

approval from his peers, and he would go to extraordinary lengths to impress them regardless of the consequences. Once he did the chemistry prep for the entire class – and it was accurate – little realizing that eighteen identical pieces of homework would obviously arouse suspicions and land him in trouble.

'On a skiing trip he managed to bed a girl, but did it in the bunk above somebody in the chalet. He thought it was a great laugh and it earned him a bit of credibility, but he was soon told there was more to getting on with people than that,' added the friend.

Roderick's best chum at Radley was Charlie Shaw, the son of legendary hard-drinking Hollywood star Robert Shaw. 'They were complete soulmates, great fun but slightly mad,' said another contemporary. 'He used to dance around the edge of the roof of his school house, hang from ledges, that sort of thing. We always thought that one day he or Charlie was going to cop it.'

Charlie is now in California selling furniture from a showroom in Los Angeles, and has little time for his old school friend. 'I have enough troubles of my own without worrying about anybody else's,' he commented.

Unlike Charlie, Roderick had his eyes fixed on joining the school's regiment, the Royal Green Jackets, regarded as elite and fashionable as the Guards. He actually seemed to enjoy the mind-bendingly boring drill of the school's compulsory cadet force and he stayed on an extra year in the sixth form to become an

NCO. 'Why on earth do you want to join the army?' he was once asked. 'Because I want to kill people,' he replied coldly.

As usual, Mark was completely the opposite of Roderick. He shied away from girls, had no interest in sport, he was arrogant, aloof and extremely unpopular. In his late teens he dismissed his parents, in a conversation with Maureen Ellam, as being 'grossly negligent and utterly incompetent', and he treated all those he met at Radley in a similarly contemptuous manner.

'He really was that bad, horrendously arrogant and extremely unpleasant,' remembers a fellow pupil of the social where Mark became head boy. 'We thought he was a bit of a psychopath; he used to have fits of anger when he would punch holes through the plasterboard walls with his bare fist. I remember once he was so scared of being set on by the other boys that he walked around with a leather strap wrapped round his fist like a knuckle duster. I think he was roughed up by the bigger boys when he first arrived and he never forgot it.'

By Radley standards the brothers were certainly not out of the top drawer when it came to status and wealth – but Mark was going to put that right. Money, and the lifestyle it bought, was to become his passion.

Roderick's unruly behaviour at Radley upset the disciplinarian side of his father, who was appalled at his pranks, and it led to a little-known episode in his life: a one-way ticket to Australia. Arriving home in the summer of 1982, expecting praise for passing his 'A' levels, he was bluntly told – go away and earn a living.

But he was in Australia only for a few months before becoming disillusioned and returning to Britain – not to Jersey or Spain for parental advice and encouragement but, via his relatives in Scotland, to a remote and rugged outward bound training centre in the far north, run by the round-the-world yachtsman John Ridgeway at Ardmore.

It was then that Elizabeth stepped in and guided him back to his chosen career, persuading him to make a successful application to Sandhurst in 1983. But just as at Radley, Roderick was never quite accepted as having the character and presence of a proper subaltern in the Royal Green Jackets. But how he tried. Stationed at Trenchard Barracks at Celle, in one of the more beautiful parts of Lower Saxony, a brother officer remembers him having 'one of these little Toyota things, a red Corolla, I think. This did not accord with the conventional Green Jacket idea of what was acceptable as an officer's car, but my word, Roderick did put it to exceptional use none the less. He liked to impress by driving at 140 m.p.h. in fog and then doing handbrake turns on the *autobahn* to Hamburg. There was much talk in the mess about these terrifying drives and Roderick adored being the centre of such derring-do.'

His water-skiing was less successful, the officer

recalls. 'He took a soldier out on the Wieser but forgot how narrow it was at that point. He did a flashy turn and the poor fellow ended up on the bank, quite badly hurt.' He earned more credibility, though, by being selected for the regiment's winter expedition to St Moritz shortly before he was to resign his commission. His stay in the swank Alpine resort, to take part in the annual 'Swift and Bold' regimental handicap, a highlight in the Green Jackets' social calender, was marked by a hair-raising descent of the Cresta Run on a tea tray. He spared no one his account of that feat during après-ski in the St Moritz tobogganing club. But members had to admit that his series of runs by the more orthodox route were impressive, particularly by someone who had fallen the previous year. The speed lover recorded 50.74 seconds, one of the best times by any Green Jacket that winter.

At the regiment's headquarters in Winchester he is remembered as the 'sandy blond with eyebrows as fair as his hair, broad, fit and slightly squat'. But he was also described as 'immensely charming', at least to many of the female 'seagulls', the dismissive title given to the pretty young things who followed the officer pack and did so much to earn Roderick the not wholly flattering nickname 'Rod the Nob'.

Another officer who knew him well summed up his army career: 'Roderick always seemed to be showing off; he was better at playing soldiers than actually being one.'

And play he did. Three months before the murders, the red Toyota which had so offended the sensibilities of his highbrow fellow officers was mysteriously torched and burned out when it was parked no more than fifty yards from the barracks guardhouse, which was on its normal high level of security alert against terrorist attack. Roderick's passport was destroyed in the blaze, but what else was in his car? Given his drug habit, there are many who speculate that the fire was precipitated by Roderick welching on an internal drugs deal.

He was a regular user of cannabis, and was later to experiment with harder drugs. Nine months later, in April 1988, he found himself in Jersey prison after being sentenced to four weeks for possessing and importing cannabis, discovered in his luggage at Jersey airport. The Newalls' family lawyer, David Le Quesne, told the court that Roderick had been under pressure from 'the tragedy' of his missing parents and as a result of his decision to quit the Green Jackets.

Meanwhile, Mark was making money while Roderick was playing at soldiers. He made a rapid and successful start as a yuppie broker, impressing the staid bankers on the money-orientated tax haven. Within eighteen months of arriving at Sheppards, after leaving school, he transferred to the City of London and on to the Banque Arabe et Internationale d'Investment.

By the time he was arrested five years later, the

elegantly-dressed young broker had built up a fund with a colleague that became one of the most successful in Paris and which, with bonuses, was earning him in excess of £150,000 a year. In the French capital, where he moved in 1992, he set up a bachelor apartment close to the Arc de Triomphe which would have been the envy of all those who had once looked down on him. He always flew club class, and if it was business in New York, he travelled by Air France Concorde. He had an account at Harrods, a personal shirt maker and a regular reservation at Blakes when he was in London. When he first moved to Paris, he stayed at the Intercontinental and dined at the Ritz, where he was a member of the health club. He worked out and practised martial arts with an instructor, in order to maintain a figure to fit his sharp suits rather than from any love of sport. Wealth was his only passion, despite the temptations of Parisian life.

Work colleagues never found any trace of a lover. Indeed, he would have had little time to spare. After regular hours at the office he would walk to his penthouse and there he would sit at his computer well into the night keeping in touch with the stockmarkets in Japan, Hong Kong, Singapore and Australia. 'Mark sometimes worked fourteen to sixteen hours a day, just to make money,' said one of his colleagues.

He was so devoted to advancing his career and impressing the banking world that he spent his last two Christmases of freedom as a guest at his boss's home. If there was any relaxation in Paris, it was the occasional visit to English-type pubs, where he would sip Guinness and look around contemptuously at the 'common' clientele.

'The brothers were completely different, in my opinion. Roderick was outgoing with no apparent desire to make more money – almost a rough type in comparison to Mark,' said one police officer who devoted months to uncovering their backgrounds. 'But the opposites did eventually attract, and for six years they were partners in crime.'

6

Miss Marple

The contribution of Maureen Ellam to bringing the brothers to court, and subsequently to long prison sentences, was recognized by Desmond de Silva, the enormously effective Crown QC in the final Gibraltar extradition hearing, when he described her as having 'something of a Miss Marple about her'.

Despite her boundless enthusiasm in keeping police fully committed when their own interest was flagging, she is now distressed and tearful and she rarely ventures out from the Crow's Nest, which she and her husband David have transformed into one of the most beautiful homes on the island, compared with the 'pigsty' that she says Nicholas and Elizabeth had left it.

She has a deep affection for all four players in the stark family tragedy, and she feels that she might have prevented it by doing more to mend the discord between them. 'I truthfully loved four people and I feel I have lost four people. If I went to the prison today and saw the boys, my reaction would be to give them a kiss and a hug and say, "I am sorry I did not understand. I should have helped you more." That is how I feel,' she said.

As she sat in what she calls 'my den' – a day room with windows on three sides providing views out over the sands and the sea and up the grassy valley where her closest friends on the island had lain in their secret grave for six years, the tears welled up in her eyes. 'Everything in me wants to help the boys. Mark needs medical help; he is mentally wrong. Roderick needs punishment, because he is a naughty boy. But let it not take over the rest of their lives.'

Turning to each one of the Newall family, she was both quick to praise and to point out faults. The strange contrast she drew is of a happy couple – 'the best marriage I have ever known' – who treated their sons so coldly that 'if you treated your dog like the two treated Mark you would be reported to the RSPCA'.

Of Elizabeth she says, 'A very beautiful woman, a big child. She never really grew up; you could imagine her reading books by Enid Blyton. She always needed soothing and I was able to do that, that was something big between us. I was always able to say, "Oh come on, now. It is not that important." She was excitable and naturally aggressive and was without doubt a spendthrift. They travelled a lot and, although she was not over-fashion-conscious, she always went to the best stores to buy clothes.'

'Nicholas,' she says, 'was arrogant, pompous – all those things that you hate until he decided that he liked you and took down the barriers, and then you could see what a lovely man he was inside. He loved us. I have a very practical husband who can do anything, a very laid-back man, no snob values, so of course Nick was instantly fascinated by him. Nick had a quite beautiful voice, like Ted Hughes the Poet Laureate, the same sort of voice, although one was a Scot and the other a Yorkshireman. The first time I saw the Crow's Nest in 1986 I asked if it got enough sunshine, as it was on the north coast. He replied in a loud voice, "I hope you know that we brought our children up there."

'I said to my husband that I was not going to like that man. What a pig! Anyway, we came down and I began to sense the humour in the man. The house was in an awful state, so awful it was a joke. And it was far too much money. But there were not many like it in Jersey with sea views and country views, so we bought it.

'Our friendship was one of the best cases of liking people for their faults. Nicholas was the most inadequate man I have ever known; he could not have done anything. He tried a bit of everything but he was really a man who did nothing.'

Maureen was captivated by Mark from the first

moment she met the boys. She had come to the Crow's Nest to inspect the property, and the two boys – then 19 and 20 – were there to show her around. 'He said nothing. He just stood there and looked – with dark hair and big glasses, he was beautiful,' she said. 'I was stunned by this young man who was like a big 10-year-old but dressed in a beautiful suit, waistcoat, collar and tie with beautifully cut hair. I thought, "What a beautiful child." I was fascinated.

'The other boy amused me by racing round, taking a great deal of trouble to show us everything. All this time the dark one said nothing and I was mesmerized by the beauty of this dark boy. The other one was handsome, but not like him.

'It was then that I said, "Are you two brothers?" The dark one opened his mouth for the first time and said, "Unfortunately, yes."

'No one will ever know what sort of young man Mark is – he is a man who is hungry for love, who has been put down all his life, and is so completely and utterly arrogant it is quite unbelievable. I never saw Mark smile, even when I praised him and he never reflected it. Nothing moved him, possibly because he was negotiating the sale of the house himself and was dealing with the money.'

Looking out now from her den windows across the valley, Maureen remembers her first confrontation with Mark back in 1986, after he had said that he considered his parents to be incompetents in selling the house. 'Now I was not going to have that from a 19-year-old. So I looked in horror at him and said, "Now come on Mark, your parents are college-educated." "That is why I have got rid of them. They are not like you and me," he replied. Well, he looked at me as though I had just crawled out of a piece of cheese. Nevertheless, he was super, super-efficient.

'I don't think Mark was starved of affection, because I just don't think he ever had any. His Aunt Nan loved him, but as for his parents . . . Elizabeth ranted and raved about him the whole time. I didn't think it was fair. But you have to remember his arrogance was quite beyond belief.

'Before we bought the Crow's Nest we knew that the Newalls and others had opposed a hotel at the end of the road putting in a clock golf layout. But when we moved in, Mark went to the hotelier and said, "Right, we have sold the house for twice what it is worth; now you can put your clock golf in." The hotelier was so angry that he came to tell us: "Cor . . . what a little shit." I replied, "Well, they grow up don't they!" Mark was not just arrogant, he seethed with deep-down hatred. I am not sure that I believe in good or evil. But if there is such a thing as evil then Mark has got a big dash of it. He has inherited big chunks of it somewhere along the line. There was big, deep-down hatred; he would think about something, withdraw from the world and one day decide he was going to do it.'

Roderick never made the same impression on her in

those early days. And when he joined the army she rarely saw him. But afterwards, as the hunt went on in the nearby woods for the bodies in 1987 and 1988, he seemed always to be nearby.

'Roderick was like Elizabeth, he too lived on a high, never thinking of the consequences of anything else. "What a fantastic thing to do," he would think. Then he would decide, "I will do that," ' said Maureen. 'And the ultimate excitement for Roderick would be for him to kill his parents.' Again her tears were not far away.

Looking back, she can pinpoint when the brothers' attitude to each other changed. It was the time of the murders. 'Then Roderick became very protective of Mark. When I was at the Newall home with the police, Mark would not look at me. But Roderick, who had met me only a couple of times, ran across the kitchen and gave me a kiss. Mark turned his back on me and could not look at me,' she recalled.

'After that, Roderick began to come here quite a lot. I think now it was because he could see where his parents were buried. He needed someone to talk to, and probably wanted to know what I knew. He was really excited about the search for his parents' bodies. He would come to me and say, "Where are the police now?" and I would say, "Up that way, I think." He would reply, "Where is that, where is that?"'

'Roderick was continually here; this was his watchtower, his nest, and he used to stand on the other side of the hill and look. I don't know if he wanted to be near his parents; more likely he was on a high.'

Even in those early days, when the brothers built an impenetrable wall against police questioning, Maureen spotted a hint of weakness in Roderick. 'I did see remorse though – defiance, but a little remorse,' she recalls. 'He was here one day in early 1988 when a little helicopter came down in the car park of the pub. Roderick came rushing in and said, "What is that, why is it here?" He was very alarmed. What he was trying to tell me, but could not say, was that his parents were buried somewhere near here.

'It would have been the perfect murder: Roderick killing his parents and Mark helping to bury them and get rid of the evidence. Perfect if Roderick could have lived with it. But I knew then that he could not. Yes, it was brilliantly done, it was brilliant in its simplicity. Of course we had all those rumours – hitmen, mafia, drug runners. But I always said no. It was just those two boys involved on their own. I think that Mark and Roderick made a suicide pact for if they were caught on the night of the murder.'

Many senior police officers came to the Crow's Nest to drink Maureen's tea or something stronger, seek her views and even ask for assistance, particularly after Roderick had been around. One of them was DCS John Saunders, head of Suffolk CID, who was called in to review the entire investigation in April 1988.

'He asked me to ask Roderick if he had murdered

his parents. Next time Roderick came I just did not know what to do. I gave him a hug and said that I could not see the point of throwing away two more lives. The only advice I could give was to get the hell off this island and never come back,' she said. 'He kept quiet the whole time. I just wanted him to know what I thought.'

Three years later, Jersey detectives Paul Marks and Jim Adamson brought an FBI agent to the Crow's Nest to ask her about her thoughts. 'He specialized in locating buried bodies and asked me why I believed the Newalls were buried in Grève de Lecq. I replied, "Lots of reasons," but told him the main one was: why did Roderick answer the door to me when they were cleaning up after the murders? And why did Mark come over here when he heard that the woods above Grève de Lecq were on fire? There are so many whys, and the real reason is that they knew every inch of the ground, where they would be disturbed and where they would not. And the agent agreed with me.'

As for motive, Maureen has little doubt that hate came first but that money was the catalyst. 'All their lives, Roderick had had violent rows with his mother and Mark with his father – there was hatred between the two. Nick was utterly cold towards them both – they did not exist to him apart from white knuckles and real hate, particularly towards Mark. You would see Mark with white knuckles also.

'Elizabeth also hated Mark. I do not think that the

boys ever had any real affection from their parents. Nick was very demanding. He needed a lot of attention and he got it from Elizabeth, so much so that it caused this huge divide with their children.

'They did not do it simply for the money. But they had watched their parents going through every bequest, every inheritance, and even selling this house, which had great potential, to buy the other one, which had nothing.

'I see many rich people on this island, and the idea is generally that if you inherit something you choose to add to it and pass it on to your children. Nick and Elizabeth were not like that. When money came to them that was the end of the line; they were going to spend it – no way were they making any provision for their offspring.'

Just a month before the murders, Uncle Kenneth in Sark decided to dispose of the bulk of his wealth before he died. Nick and his brother Stephen were each given half a million pounds, which would go to their children when they died. A month later they were dead.

'Now whether they were given money, shares or an interest of a trust fund, I do not know. But suffice to say we had a night out with Nick and Elizabeth to celebrate.'

Maureen was so close to the victims that she had two dreams soon after the murders, which would have been nightmares to anyone else. 'The first vision caused me no fear. I clearly saw Nick before I woke up and there he was on his knees at the door to the french windows which lead to the bedroom terrace. He was dressed. Even though he had blood running down his face it was not a nightmare. Why should it be? I loved him and his wife. I shouted, "Nick, oh Nick", and I put my hands out towards him. His left hand was scratching the glass. I feel now that that hand was not pointing to the woods above the house as I believed it was then, but down to the valley where the grave was later to be found . . . he was trying to tell me where he and Elizabeth were. The vision confirmed what I already knew: that they had been murdered and buried.

'Mentally, I was getting into a very bad state; you think you know the answers, but you are not really sure. Then I had my second vision and it was weird. I was in the back of the bus or a coach travelling somewhere – I think we were alongside a bay like the one outside the house. Coming towards me across the bay was a boat. I saw it was Nick's boat. Elizabeth was at the helm, Nick was sitting back with his pipe. She had her glasses around her neck as she always did; slightly behind her was Mark. She waved to me and she was smiling. Then she shouted, "We are all right," and then there was a pause before she added, "Let it be." Those were her exact words.'

Eerily, this echoed almost exactly a dream that Aunt Nan Clark had on 10 October 1987 – the night of the murder, according to the account of Desmond de Silva QC in Gibraltar. 'Roderick,' the barrister told the court, 'asked if his mother had ever appeared to her in a dream. She said, "Yes, the night she died." To this, Roderick posed the question, "What did she say?" She told him that in that nightmare his mother had said, "I told you he meant it and I told you it would happen, but let the matter rest." '

Said Maureen, 'I did not know that Nan had had the same message. But I thought then: "I have just got to live with this." These were four people who had so much, they were so much fun and now all are destroyed – what a waste, what a chronic waste.

'Nick would come up the hill on a tiny little machine, like a toy motorbike. He looked so funny and I would say, "Come on, give me a lift."

'If we all had courage, we would live the way Nick and Elizabeth lived. Yes, they had lots of faults, yes they did owe the boys a lot more than they gave them. And yes, they should have bothered a lot more about them. I do not want to see these boys spend so much of their lives in prison; what does it achieve? Please God, life should not mean life in prison. It will not bring the other two back.'

And the tears once again started to flood her eyes.

7

Needle in a Haystack

From the start, the police investigation was marked by hard grafting work at grass-root level but a lack of interest and sometimes even apathy at the highest level. For increasingly frustrated detectives it seemed that every lead produced too few breaks and too many blind alleys and red herrings.

One such false lead was the pink Mercedes. It had been reported as having been seen in the area at the time of the murders, but detectives soon ruled it out. Yet for some reason it was included in an appeal on the TV programme 'Crimewatch UK' a month after the murders. The programme, with its huge audience, has done much to help solve many of Britain's most gruesome crimes, notably Michael Sams's kidnaps and murder and the James Bulger child killing in Liverpool.

The 'Crimewatch' programme went out on 10 November 1987 and viewers responded with fifty phone calls, several of them wasted on the bogus pink

Mercedes. Nothing came of any of them. A few days after the 'Crimewatch' programme, Roderick's eyes almost popped out of his head and brother Mark was white with rage when they spotted detectives Adamson and Nimmo mingling with the family mourners at Uncle Kenneth's funeral in Guernsey.

Their tempers got no better during the wake at the Old Government House Hotel. Stephen Newall put pressure on the two boys to return to Jersey for further questioning. Both had been giving the island a wide berth since the murders.

Stephen did not mince his words. He told them to start co-operating with the police. It was their father and mother and his brother and sister-in-law who were missing, and they were not doing enough to help. Roderick made excuses, saying he had to return to his regiment, but after another stern lecture from Stephen, both he and Mark finally agreed to return to Jersey later that week. Understandably, both were far from happy about the prospect of further questioning.

When the interviews did finally take place the detectives decided the brothers should be questioned separately. Roderick, always suspicious of the investigators, brought his own tape recorder, which he placed on the table in front of him and ostentatiously switched on. The atmosphere of confrontation continued at lunch at Mark's favourite restaurant, Victoria's at the Grand Hotel in St Helier. Adamson and Nimmo sat between the brothers, eating steak and chips and sipping mineral water. They did not talk during the meal about the case and they did not enjoy the food. The tension was almost unbearable as the detectives strained to ensure there was no secret contact between Roderick and Mark.

These sessions in the interview room at Rouge Bouill were the longest confrontation between the brothers and the detectives who were pursuing them until – many years later – they were finally to admit their guilt. The officers grilled Roderick for eight hours and then went straight into five hours of interviews with Mark. The sessions finished at 1 a.m. There were discrepancies between the brothers' accounts: for example, they could not agree what type of sauce had been on the scampi for the Sunday lunch they claimed they had shared with their parents the day after the murders, but this was hardly an admission of guilt, and from the brothers' point of view their paramount aim of keeping their guilt hidden had been successfully achieved. Their carefully-worked-out alibi was still watertight. In fact Roderick had even gone on the attack, accusing the police of dishonesty and demanding to see papers taken from his parents' Spanish villa.

Four months later, in May 1988, with Roderick on the verge of leaving the Royal Green Jackets and setting off on his father's yacht *Chanson de Lecq*, possibly never to return, the police called the brothers in together to police headquarters for one last attempt to break them down. They did not bat an eyelid as Roderick was accused of lifting the carpet in the bedroom where Maureen Ellam had pointed out the tell-tale stain which she had thought was coffee but which subsequently proved to be blood from his mother's head. Yes, admitted Roderick in an obviously cool and clearly-thought-out reply, he had indeed nailed down the carpet, but that was months before his parents went missing, when they had complained that it had been catching on the bedroom door.

Meanwhile, in the so far fruitless search for the missing corpses a new technique of sub-level radar was brought in from Scotland to help. The search was now stretching to most corners of the forty square miles that make up the island. The new equipment which, said one officer, 'looked impressive enough, but was not very successful', was used to scour the garden of the family home and other suspected areas.

However, the police were on the verge of their biggest break. On a windy day in March 1988, police dog handler Phil Kirkham from the Greater Manchester force had brought his two alsatians to the island. The dogs had helped in the successful hunt for a Moors murder victim who had lain buried under Saddleworth Moor for twenty years. This time the dogs did not find bodies, but they did discover the remains of Roderick and Mark's bonfire of evidence. In the ashes were the two lenses from Nicholas's glasses – unique to him, so that they were almost as good as a fingerprint. The victim's opticians confirmed they could not possibly belong to anyone else.

There was also the remains of Elizabeth's handbag, with her pen and perfume bottle, part of Nicholas's pipe and fragments of a book on French restaurants with comments in the margins written by Nick's mother Sheila. But the most damaging piece of evidence was a Bissell upholstery brush, containing a tuft of fibre from the lounge carpet at 9 Clos de l'Atlantique and other fibres from the fawn carpet in the master bedroom. Also among the debris were other traces of the brothers' clean-up operation, including fabrics of J cloth taken from the kitchen.

Detectives gave details of the find at a press conference, but the location, just above the Crow's Nest, was deliberately withheld. Someone knew where it was, however, and could not resist turning up. To the surprise of no one among the investigators, it was Roderick.

The next month, police found one of the spades the mystery man with the Teutonic accent had bought at the hardware store in St Helier as part of what the police suspected could have been Roderick's 'murder and burial kit'. It was discovered at Noirmont Common, close to where the brothers had asked their neighbours the Bickertons if they could burn some rubbish. Anger was mounting on the island that the brothers were still happily walking around free in the face of the mounting evidence against them. But with no bodies and no confession, there was no way an arrest warrant could be signed.

By now Roderick, thoroughly alarmed, was in Spain preparing his father's boat for his voyages, which were to take him half a world away from Jersey. An attempt to serve an arrest warrant now would involve an international operation.

Meanwhile, police efforts to find new evidence were intensifying. Home Office scientist Ken Creere and a team from the Metropolitan Police were brought over, literally to take the murder house to pieces. Creere, an expert in laser fingerprinting, removed all the wallpaper and the entire ceiling from the lounge to take back to London for tests. No new evidence was found.

The months ticked by through 1988 and 1989. The incident room was wound down. There were plenty of theories on the island, of course, where the murders were still the number-one topic for rumour, but no new evidence.

While Mark was in Paris making his reputation as a shrewd broker and building his fortune, Roderick was sailing way out of reach, building a reputation as a skilled yachtsman. The case seemed dead and buried.

In 1990, detectives Adamson and Martin Fitzgerald were finally given permission to review the Newall murders and Nan Clark flew to Jersey to lend the support of the family. As always Maureen Ellam up at the Crow's Nest and Angela Barnes watched like hawks urging the police to greater effort and keeping an ever open ear to the grapevine. Could something new be found?

It was over two years since the murders. Adamson and Fitzgerald drove with Nan Clark back to Clos de l'Atlantique. As Adamson told Nan that night, 'It was like going back into the past. Everything had been left as it was in October 1987.' In the lounge there were still that month's copies of Nicholas and Elizabeth's favourite magazines, *Boat Owner, Country, Your Money* and *Toyota Today*, reflecting the focus of the murdered middle-aged couple's interest in spending money. But at the end of the review there was still no new evidence.

One cold and wet day that February, the detectives were searching the fields at the back of the Crow's Nest. They felt they were in the right area, but again their search had been in vain. Adamson told his colleagues, 'We have to keep searching, we just need one break of luck. But to be honest it is like looking for a needle in a haystack. In fact we are still looking for the haystack.'

They had found no new evidence, they were no closer to solving the murders and time was against them. With the lack of progress, the States police chiefs were losing interest in the whole matter and the investigation was close to being wound up. On April Fools' Day 1990 the detectives submitted their report. The only conclusion was that a lack of evidence had to mean no arrests. This was the news the brothers wanted; now the money would be theirs.

On a chilly January morning in 1991, Mark Newall arrived at the Royal Court of Jersey in St Helier with advocate David Le Quesne and barrister Peter Barnes for what the murder accomplice believed would be the final hurdle between him and the perfect crime. Bailiff Sir Peter Crill would declare his parents officially dead, clearing the way for the brothers to inherit their parents' wealth.

Mark, in his characteristic City suit and tie, was the first witness, and he gave a cool and fluent rendition of the cover story, finishing with the brothers leaving the island for the UK after the entirely fictitious pleasant Sunday lunch with their parents. 'I have never seen them since,' he told a court packed not only with intrigued islanders, but with hordes of press from London, where the murder mystery story had taken a grip on the headlines. Mark added solemnly, 'I believe they are dead primarily for three reasons. I have not seen or heard from them for more than three years. I have seen no evidence that they have used any of their financial assets in those three years. And also largely because of information given to me by the police, who have indicated that they are investigating murder.'

Mr Barnes told the Bailiff that Roderick was unable to be in court because he was in the Falklands.

Detective Superintendent Martyn Le Brocq said he believed the Newalls had been killed. 'Because of a very thorough clean-up which the property had been given, bloodstains had not immediately been apparent at the start of the investigation,' he explained.

The hearing took just half an hour, but the police were not going to let Mark get away with it that easily, and so they made one last effort to crack him. He was taken back to headquarters past the dozens of press and television cameras camped outside. There, Adamson and Fitzgerald grilled him for seven hours. He was accused directly of murdering his parents and told that all the evidence pointed to him and Roderick carrying out the killing after the dinner at the Sea Crest. As if responding to a business proposition, Mark coolly replied that he intended to go away and consult Roderick and other members of the family before responding.

The next day, Adamson met Mark outside his parents' house and formally handed over the keys to the murder scene. With his parents officially declared dead, and the inheritance on its way, Mark decided he no longer had to take any more questioning from the police. Summoning the detectives back to his parents' house, he told them in front of Nan and Alastair Clark that Roderick had no intention of returning from the Falklands and that they would not speak to the police again on the matter.

The wills of Nick and Elizabeth Newall were published four months later. They had made separate testaments on 20 October 1986, just under a year before they were to die, each leaving everything to the other. The documents contained the proviso that in the event of both dying the full estates were to be equally divided between their sons. Not even the police know just how much each estate was worth, but most estimate that Roderick and Mark were jointly some £800,000 better off.

8

A Gentleman of Leisure

By the time the inheritance came through, Roderick had been out of the reach of Jersey police for almost three years. Buying himself out of the army, he had taken Maureen Ellam's advice to 'get the hell out of the island and never come back'.

After a memorable farewell bash with his fellow officers at the Royal Green Jackets headquarters in Winchester, he headed straight for Javea in Spain in May 1988 to prepare his father's yacht, to sail the world and to try to erase from his conscience the terrible events in Jersey just seven months earlier. Roderick's intention first to take on the Atlantic single-handed was hazardous, if not reckless, for a sailor whose experience was limited to holiday sailing around the Jersey waters. Later, some of those murder squad detectives who were yachtsmen themselves admitted a grudging respect for Roderick's achievements in sailing in some of the most dangerous waters in the world.

But it was another challenge, another dare. One senior Jersey officer said that it was his belief that Roderick took to the oceans not really caring if he was swallowed up in the storms. In those four years of self-imposed exile, Roderick became, in the words of Desmond de Silva, 'a gentleman of leisure'.

Travelling the world, the blond, athletic former public schoolboy with the army background, invariably dressed in a navy-blue yachting blazer, charmed everyone he met, from the snooty set haunting New Zealand's most exclusive marinas to the sheep farmers and that rare and strange breed of ex-pats, who for whatever reason had sold up and settled in the Falkland Islands. Roderick fitted in perfectly.

For months on end, alone with his boat and his memories, he negotiated the storms and the doldrums of the Atlantic and the Pacific. There were no phone calls, letters or even a postcard to friends or relatives alike. His one contact was his brother, Mark, who would occasionally receive the odd line on Roderick's whereabouts.

This odyssey or escape from justice took Roderick from Javea down the Spanish coast, and across the Straits of Gibraltar to Tangier on the north Moroccan coast. Taking on more supplies, he then completed the dream of so many yachtsmen: the single-handed run across the Atlantic. Passing through the Panama Canal, he called in at various Pacific islands before reaching New Zealand. On the other side of the world from Jersey, he felt safe enough to mingle and relax for the first time since that goodbye party in Winchester.

He berthed at the Westpark Marina on the upper Waltemata Harbour and wandered into the bar of the Hobsonville Return Services Association Club. To the club's Honorary Secretary, Tom Palmer, it was natural that the Royal Green Jackets officer should be made welcome without asking any further questions. After all, as he explained, 'That was the way between the services the world over. What was more,' said Mr Palmer, 'everyone at the club thought he was a "nice bloke".' He added, 'He was a very well-presented young man, well-spoken, public school and very personable.'

Roderick spent several months among his new friends in New Zealand, sometimes staying with Mr Palmer, his wife Ann, and their two children Stacey and Thomas, and sometimes on his boat or with other friends. He felt so comfortable that he even began talking about his parents, telling Mr Palmer that they had disappeared in Jersey.

'He said he and his brother had been grilled about them and that, without any doubt, they had been murdered. He was obviously distressed about this horrendous experience and was struggling within himself to come to terms with the fact that his parents were gone and to get back to living his own life again. To be honest, I felt nothing but sympathy for this young man's tragedy and Roderick endeared himself to us much more. We never thought for a second that this nice bloke had it within him to have murdered his mum and dad.'

When, at Christmas 1989, Roderick started preparing his yacht to face the oceans once again, with the Falklands his next destination, there was an air of sadness around the marina and the club. 'He did not mention anything about an inheritance, but even at that stage he appeared to have a pot of dough. He was a generous man at the bar, always standing his round. We like to see that here at the club,' adds Palmer. 'He was that type of person, one of the most popular guests we have had for a long time. So when I received a phone call from a Jersey officer two and a half years later, I remembered Roderick right away and was still prepared to give him the benefit of the doubt. After all, a man is innocent until proved guilty, regardless of what he is charged with.'

Palmer remembers saying to the detective: 'You are not Bergerac, are you?' and hearing a groan at the other end of the line. This is not a popular opening remark to make to any Jersey policeman; they are all heartily sick and tired of the fictional sleuth.

Neither the Newalls nor the police had any idea where Roderick could possibly be during most of 1990. Jersey police were not to see him from May 1988 until his return to Britain in July 1992. When he sailed off with so little ocean-going sailing experience they thought he had a death wish and frankly did not give two hoots if he killed himself. Yet, almost despite himself, he made it.

And by the time he nosed the *Chanson de Lecq* out of Auckland harbour, he was no longer single-handed. He had taken on crew, a soulmate and a lover, all in the person of Donna Westend. An attractive 25-year-old divorcee, he had met her at a quayside barbecue. Both were lonely; Roderick was looking for the comfort of a more experienced woman and she was taken in by the boyish good looks of this wealthy young adventurer with no ties and commitments. They were to have a tempestuous and at times violent relationship. But when they parted it was as close friends. They still exchange letters between prison and New Zealand.

Now working in a post office in Whangarei, Donna has no regrets about sharing part of her life with a man she now knows to be a double parent killer. She refuses either to condemn him or to reveal anything about the intimacies between them. 'All I want to do is keep out of the limelight. I am sick of people pointing me out or trying to force me to talk about Roderick. I have been hounded and harassed,' she complains. 'Loving him and travelling with him was part of my life, and I look upon it as an experience. I certainly do not have anything against him. He had his reasons for doing what he did, even if it was killing his parents, and it is not for me to judge him for it. He was good to me at the time, and I never thought he could be capable of murder. In the end no harm came to me and I returned safely.'

Donna hinted at a curious mix of love and latent violence that marked their stormy affair and which indicated the extreme moods of which Roderick was capable. 'A thirty-two-foot boat is not a lot of space for two people of very different character to get along in without conflict. When you are together in such cramped space you go through all the emotions,' she said. 'He was quick-tempered, but I can be quite fiery too. I look back and quite scare myself by remembering that if I had had enough confidence and I felt I could handle the boat myself, I would have given Rod a really good push, sending him flying overboard. And I know that there were times he felt the urge to do the same to me.'

Roderick's propensity for violence against vulnerable defenceless people who upset him was clearly shown when the yacht docked at Port Stanley. Donna disembarked with her pretty face bearing the scars and bruises of a beating.

As with others Roderick had met in New Zealand, he was not afraid to tell Donna of the family murder mystery and exactly whom the police suspected. But she refuses to say whether he confessed to her, as he was to do to his next serious girlfriend. 'I possibly suspected something – you cannot be a normal person carrying a secret like that. I just wish he had got it over with a lot quicker than going through all that legal shit in Gibraltar, which took well over a year.'

Donna eventually said goodbye to Roderick in the spring of 1991, after he had taken her to Buenos Aires in Argentina, from where she made her own way back to New Zealand. 'I still keep my photographs of him, which I am keeping to myself. It is part of my private life which will not be dragged up. From his letters, Rod says that he is being looked after now like a human being at least. It could not have been too pleasant in Gibraltar.

'I think he has gained a lot of strength from cleaning his conscience. Since his arrest, he expected to get twenty-five years plus. But he is looking forward to the future, not dwelling on what has happened in the past.

'He is guarded in his letters, because he fears they are being read before they leave the prison. I have lost a lot of faith in people over this whole affair. People have twisted things about Rod – all I know is that he has got to have gone through something pretty dramatic to have done something like that.

'Rod has made peace with himself at last, and thank goodness for that.

'We were from worlds apart, but I will never forget him.'

Life in the Falklands could not have been in starker contrast to the gin-and-tonic, back-slapping company in the New Zealand marinas. Roderick's army survival training was invaluable in adapting to the rugged and inhospitable islands. They reminded him of the bleak Scottish Highlands, where he had taken part in John Ridgeway's adventure training course. But the company was very different.

In Port Stanley he fell in with the *Black Pig* crowd, named after the rusty old tug owned by Steven Beldham, a new friend who was to become Roderick's regular crewman. The *Black Pig* crowd were a bunch of hard-drinking loners who, like Roderick, did not welcome too close probing of their past. Many of them had retreated to the Falklands and turned their back on the modern world. Roderick felt at home among them.

One of the bunch was Jerome Poncet, and Roderick joined him and his wife Sally at their home on Beaver Island, which they owned. Their control over the island was so complete that they would not even let Jersey detective Martin Fitzgerald land when he made enquiries among Roderick's friends in the South Atlantic. Indeed, a complete blanket of silence was thrown over Roderick's activities in the Falklands by his friends there.

Roderick spent less than two years on the Falklands, but the friendships he made there and the opportunity to purge his memory of his past horrors made a major impression on him. At one point, he travelled even further south to the Antarctic with Poncet, where they met up with the film crew making David Attenborough's BBC TV series 'Life in the Freezer'. The film-makers were so grateful to be allowed to use

Poncet's boat, *Damien II*, crewed by Roderick, that the owner was given a credit on the closing titles of the programme when, years later, it finally reached the screen in Britain in the winter of 1993.

On Beaver Island, Poncet was 'absolutely staggered' when he heard that Roderick had admitted he had murdered his parents. 'The only time he mentioned his parents while he was staying here with me was to say that they had disappeared,' he said in a heavy French accent. 'Down here we do not ask anyone about their past. We take the view that it is no business of ours. It was clear that like so many others Roderick had arrived here to start afresh with a new lifestyle. That is not a problem.

'I do remember how friendly he was and popular. No one had a bad word to say about him. He threw himself into all the activity around the island: farming, land management, safeguarding the livestock and of course sailing.'

Poncet's fondest memories of Roderick revolve around his patience and understanding with his host's three young children. He liked to read them stories on the seemingly endless winter nights and take them on walks around the rugged island on the equally long summer days. Poncet suspected that he yearned for children of his own, although he wanted to enjoy a few more years of bachelor freedom first.

'I did not get the impression that Roderick was obsessed or disturbed with the bad treatment his parents had given him, but I did feel that he was determined that no child should be deprived of parental love in the way he clearly believed he had been,' he said.

Whatever his friendship with Roderick, Poncet is blunt in his condemnation of Roderick's explanation to the police about why he killed his mother and father. 'Roderick did tell me he had been sent away to boarding school at an early age; well, that's what happens to a lot of children in England,' he said. 'You do not hate your parents because of that. You may run away from them, but you do not go back several years later and kill them.'

He confirmed that Roderick was extremely happy in the Falklands and says he had every intention of returning to set up a permanent home in the islands. 'He definitely wanted that; he never looked on it as being grim, that is a wrong perception. Roderick knew that life here is perfectly manageable with experience and he peeled away any preconceived reservations and came to terms with it all.

'He was on his way back to the Falklands when he was arrested and taken to Gibraltar. He had told me that once he had got his new yacht he would be coming back for ever. When he gets out, he will be only as old as I am now – in his forties – and he will get a warm welcome from everyone here in the Falklands if he still wants to come back.'

But eventually Roderick's wanderlust, and the

promptings of Donna, were to lead him away. He headed for South America where, his relationship now over, he said goodbye to Donna and, instead, sailed straight into another romance, one which was finally to lead to his downfall.

After months at sea, he sailed into the Brazilian port of Pôrto Alegre, meaning the Port of Happiness, and met 35-year-old Brazilian divorcee and English teacher Helena Pedo. After tying up at the private Beleiros do Sol Yacht Club, the most exclusive in Brazil's sixth largest city, he walked into the clubhouse looking like a Viking, with long scruffy hair and a gingerish goatee beard.

Helena, whose three teenaged children lived with her former accountant husband, sensed the attractive features and bearing of the young Englishman. They were introduced within moments. Helena was called over to help with the language barrier and they got on so well that she invited him to her friend Eloisa Endres's 30th birthday party that night.

Helena never left his side all night. They talked until dawn and the relationship which was to prove fatal to Roderick's hopes of escaping justice was born. Despite the burgeoning love that night, not everyone was happy about the arrival of the English stranger. Eloisa's boyfriend sensed danger and told her 'this guy is trouble'. Eloisa, delighted to see her friend Helena so happy, dismissed the warning.

Within a few weeks, early in 1991, Roderick invited

the two girls out for a champagne dinner. Helena was puzzled: what was there to celebrate? 'I have become a millionaire,' he replied with a smirk of self-satisfaction – he had just learned that his inheritance had come through.

Eloisa was to say of Roderick's relationship with Helena: 'He wanted to marry her for love, but I think there was another reason for him wanting to settle here. He knew, just like the English train robber Ronnie Biggs, that if he married a Brazilian girl and had children they would never be able to take him back to face the courts.'

With his new wealth, Roderick planned to set up a yacht charter business and throughout 1991 he was in the market for a bigger and better boat. But he was still unable to erase the memory of what he had done, nor could he control the streak of violence which was starting to frighten Helena. He became aggressive to her, there were rows and she began to wonder if her friend's warning that 'this guy is trouble' was indeed coming true.

One cold day in July – Brazil's winter – while cuddling Helena by the fire the past suddenly overcame Roderick. He was about to break. He asked her to fetch a book from the bedroom. It was the Nobel Prize-winning novel *Magister Ludi* by Hermann Hesse. Opening it at a well-thumbed page he started to read: 'Oh! he thought in grief and horror, now I am guilty of his death. And only now, when there was no longer need to save his pride or offer resistance, he felt, in shock and sorrow, how dear this man had already become to him. And since in spite of all rational objections he felt responsible for the Master's death, there came over him, with a premonitory shudder of awe, a sense that this guilt would utterly change him and his life, and would demand much greater things of him than he had ever before demanded of himself.'

With that, he began to weep, the tears streaming down his face. Shaking Helena by the shoulders, he blurted out, 'I am a murderer, I am a murderer, I am a murderer.'

Desmond de Silva described the dramatic scene in Helena Pedo's flat when she realized that her lover was a double killer. 'He spoke in terms of regret about being responsible for the killings and added that it was only after the murder that he had discovered that his parents were very much in love with each other,' he said. 'He spoke of the pain and burden of his guilt and that he had to open his heart to her because of how close she had become to him,' said the QC. The night of the confession, Roderick was told he was not welcome in Helena's bed. He slept on the couch.

Helena was to keep her secret for a year, until she was tracked down by Jersey detectives. She thought that no one would believe her if she reported what she had heard to local police in a country where a murder can be bought for as little as ten dollars. Her friend Eloisa explained, 'Roderick fell in love with her. Men are weak and do stupid things when they are in love. I think Helena believed him deep down, but was not completely sure. I do not know why she did not take action. Maybe the police would have dismissed her report. After all, it was nothing to do with anyone in Brazil.

'Helena kept asking Roderick, "Why?" But all he told her was that had never forgiven his parents for sending him away to boarding school. He told me that after boarding school there was no way out: it was either prison or the army.'

But like Donna Westend, Helena found herself remaining loyal to the lonely yachtsman. He wanted her to help him come to terms with the dreadful reality of his own guilt, and she responded. He also wanted her to meet the only other person who knew of that guilt.

In the depths of the southern hemisphere's 1992 winter he took her to the warmth of Miami and introduced her to Mark, who had flown over from Paris. She listened as Roderick discussed his future plans with his brother and shared his disappointment that a boat he had come to look over was nowhere near good enough for his new business plans. Mark warned him, as only a fellow conspirator could, never to return to Britain, even though the Jersey police seemed to have gone cold on the investigation.

That night, as Mark flew back, Roderick and Helena

went to see the Hollywood thriller *Cape Fear*, starring Robert de Niro. Helena hated the film. But as they emerged from the cinema Roderick smiled and said that he had enjoyed it because it was 'good to live in fear'.

The man whom Maureen Ellam described as constantly searching for a 'high' could sense thin ice again. He was ready to skate on it.

Roderick Newall decided to go home. Helena protested: 'Aren't you afraid of the police?' He made no reply. He had heard about what might be the perfect yacht for him, on sale in London. His 'high' would be to test the reaction of his relatives, regardless of what Mark had said.

9

His Father's Double

A fashionable leather holdall over his shoulder, Roderick stood with his feet on British soil for the first time in four years when he arrived at Heathrow in June 1992. The one thought which nagged at him as he passed through passport control was not the fear of arrest, but what his reaction would be when he stared into the face of his father's twin, Stephen. He was quite comfortable about facing all his other relatives, but seriously doubted that he could sustain the act under the glare of Uncle Stephen.

It was exactly this sense of danger that had an irresistible attraction for him. The daredevil inside him was egging him on – but he was far from certain that he could maintain his cover and resist the demands of his conscience to come clean.

First stop was to view the sixty-six-foot, twin-masted, steel-hulled *Austral Soma* at St Catherine's Dock in the shadow of Tower Bridge. He knew immediately that the boat would be perfect for his embryonic chartering business, even at the £200,000 asking price. After lengthy negotiations, he secured the sale of the Southampton-registered boat and navigated it around the coast to a less expensive berth at Brighton Marina and then on to Boulogne, where he arranged for it to be left in the trusted hands of Steven Beldham.

Returning to London, he met his best friend from Radley, Charlie Shaw, and over a lunchtime pizza was introduced to the beautiful blonde society girl Emma-Jane Lonsdale. The Newall charm had lost none of its power over the passing years, and within an hour the 29-year-old girl, well enough connected to walk arm in arm with Viscount Linley in the Royal Enclosure at Ascot, had lent him both her Fulham flat and a car for a week, while she holidayed in Italy with her boyfriend.

Emma-Jane, described in the society columns as 'Venus-proportioned', is the daughter of banker, restaurant owner and publisher Norman Lonsdale, a former 'walker' for Princess Margaret, who was once prominently but erroneously tipped to be the new husband of the Queen's sister. She herself went to art school with Lady Sarah Armstrong-Jones and has, at various times, been a part-time waitress at a Chelsea wine bar, a deep-diving instructor in the paradise Windward Island of Bequia and co-founder of a record label with Charley Boorman, star of *The Emerald Forest* and son of film director John Boorman.

After his years in exile, flitting from the return servicemen's club in New Zealand to the *Black Pig* crowd in the Falklands and the middle-class Portuguese-speaking company in Brazil, Roderick found it no trouble slipping back into and being accepted by the young Chelsea set.

'He seemed a very respectable and together sort of guy. He was upright, terribly polite and very organized and capable. After all, he has sailed halfway round the world,' said Emma-Jane. 'He was a friend of a very good friend of mine, and people have criticized me for helping someone I hardly knew. But I am just like that. He needed a place to stay for a week and I was going away for exactly that length of time. It seemed the most natural thing to do for him to stay at the flat. I was happy to let him use my car, my little VW Golf GTi. But I did not expect him to drive it to Scotland and back.'

Not far away from Roderick's temporary and free accommodation in Emma-Jane's elegant flat in Fulham's Holyport Road lived Nan Clark. There was no reason why he had to tell any of his family that he was back in Britain, particularly when the one man he feared most would be certain to find out, but in the end the temptation to visit his favourite aunt to tell her how he had been spending his new-found wealth proved too much.

He called round in July 1992 on a particularly warm summer evening. Nan was surprised, because she thought he was still in the South Atlantic, but she welcomed him in for dinner. During the evening her doctor husband was called away to an emergency and, alone together, their conversation perhaps inevitably turned to the murder mystery.

At first, Roderick maintained his well-practised routine of pretending to be baffled but, undeterred, the shrewd Nan probed deeper into Roderick's soul. The further her questions went, the more rattled he became. Suddenly he asked her if she had seen his mother in a dream. 'Yes,' his aunt replied, looking straight at him.

'What did she say?' Roderick continued nervously.

'It was a nightmare . . . your mother said to me, "I told you he meant it, I told you it would happen, but let the matter rest." Tell me, Roderick,' she continued, 'what exactly did happen that night?'

Shaken, all trace of his normal arrogance long drained away, he whispered back: 'Even if you knew exactly what happened, you would still not understand.'

Uncannily, Nan's nightmare was almost identical to the vision which had come to Maureen Ellam at the Crow's Nest, the old family home, soon after the murders.

There was no turning back for Roderick now, and before he left Nan's he promised not only to visit his grandmother in North Berwick, but also to contact Uncle Stephen. The next day he sped north in Emma-Jane's VW.

On Monday 13 July, Jim Adamson, at his desk at Rouge Bouillon, received a call from Angela Barnes. Nothing had happened on the double murder inquiry for months, if not years, and none of the detectives had much optimism left. But out of the blue Mrs Barnes provided the tip which was to bring the case dramatically back to life: Roderick was back. Mrs Barnes told him that Nan had rung to say Roderick had been back in the UK for six weeks and was on his way to Scotland. The Jersey detectives knew that if Roderick was to speak to his uncle, and if they could record the conversation, this was their one chance of the breakthrough they so desperately wanted.

Superintendent Paul Marks, head of Jersey CID, phoned the Scottish Crime Squad in Glasgow and obtained permission from the Chief Constable to tape the meeting. The only problem was: could it be arranged in time?

Adamson rang Stephen at his home in Rhu, his office and Strathclyde University, where he lectured sometimes, all without success. The Jersey detectives went home that night in anguish at still failing to track him down. It was the Scottish police who finally located Stephen at the Dunkeld House Hotel outside Perth. Stephen phoned Adamson at his home and agreed to co-operate, despite the fact that he was with his wife celebrating her 60th birthday.

First, he had to contact Roderick to lure him into the trap. After many hours of telephoning around the family, Stephen finally discovered that Roderick had just left his cousins William and Amanda Clark in Blair Drummond to return to his grandmother in North Berwick prior to driving back to London and off on his yacht. For Roderick had finally recognized that he did not have the guts to face his father's twin. As he told Helena Pedo, if he saw his Uncle Stephen he feared he would not be able to maintain his silence. And he was not going to take the risk. So he was surprised when, at his grandmother's, he picked up the phone and heard the stern voice of Stephen demanding his presence for tea at the Dunkeld House Hotel the next day.

Roderick was forced to change his plans. He would have lunch with his godmother, Lady Vanessa Prosser, wife of one of the leading figures in the Scottish legal establishment Lord William Prosser, and arrive at the Dunkeld at 3 p.m. This gave Detectives Marks and Adamson less than eighteen hours to get to Scotland.

'That night I was sure that Stephen was not going to be able to pull it off. In fact I had my doubts that Roderick would even turn up at the hotel,' said Adamson. 'It was a really bad day for Stephen. He and his wife Gay had gone for a quiet celebration, and the last thing they wanted was all this aggravation. I think they thought: "Gosh, I wish he had never phoned us." '

But the trap was set . . . as long as Roderick showed up. DCI Jim Smith of the Scottish Crime Squad met

Stephen and Gay to set up the bugging of their suite. Marks and Adamson caught the first plane to Heathrow, intending to catch a connection to Edinburgh, but the two-hour delay would have proved calamitous, so they flew to Glasgow instead, hired a car and headed into the Highlands at up to ninety miles an hour.

'We just hammered it. It was a wonder that we did not get pulled in by the local traffic squad,' remembers Marks.

10

The Sting

The Dunkeld House Hotel is a most unlikely setting for a covert police operation to trap a double murderer. The hotel is set in a 200-acre estate outside Perth in the heart of the Scottish Highlands, surrounded by land owned by the richest of the nobility in Scotland. Bugging a suite in the Edwardian country house with ninety-two bedrooms is not the usual request made to the management, who are more used to enquiries about the hotel's prime facilities for the hunting, shooting and fishing elite.

Stephen and Gay would have preferred to walk along the two-mile private beat of the River Tay, which offers some of the finest salmon and trout fishing in Scotland, rather than extracting a confession to the murder of Stephen's own brother and sister-in-law from his nephew.

Around midday, the police surveillance squad and their technical back-up arrived from Dunfermline. A mini tape recorder was hidden in the sofa where Roderick, if he was going to arrive, would sit, and several radio mikes were placed around the suite. Two doors down the corridor, the technicians set up a control centre in a small maid's room. The tests proved perfect and the trap was baited.

As the Jersey detectives neared the hotel, Jim Smith told them on their mobile phone to wait outside Dewar's Whisky Distillery. A Scottish crime squad car pulled in and both the officers transferred. Adamson was the only officer in the operation who would have been recognized by Roderick.

'I told him to lie on the floor in the back of the car. It must have been very unpleasant for Jim. He told me later that he didn't know where he was going, because all he could see was sky. Paul was in the front,' said Smith. 'We had the police radio on and the stake-out team said that Roderick had still not arrived at the hotel. So we stopped on some high ground to wait and see if he was coming in. We were all getting a bit low and I could sense that the Jersey men were thinking that it might all turn out to be a waste of time. It was decided to drive down to the hotel.'

Just as the Q car was driving up to the entrance, Roderick arrived. The officers made a fast detour into the car park with Adamson still lying on the floor of the vehicle. Smith then explained how one of his surveillance squad went to the car when it was thought to be all clear and escorted Adamson towards the hotel. He was just at the front door when he was suddenly grabbed and thrown back into the car. 'He is coming out, get in, get in,' he was warned.

Jim Smith had provided a fourteen-man surveillance squad, some hidden in the grounds, others posing as guests and at least one as a member of the hotel staff. Roderick's every move was flashed to the control room. If it had not been, he would have walked straight into the face of DI Adamson, aborting the whole operation. They had no idea why Roderick was returning suddenly to his car, just a few moments after arriving. Was he backing out of the confrontation with Stephen and Gay? Had he had a row with them? Was it panic? Or had he rumbled the trap? In fact he was just fetching a brochure from the car, and so the police officers breathed again.

Adamson was back lying as close as possible to the floor of the police car. The detective later told his Scottish colleagues that he had thought, 'Bloody hell, what is going to happen if Roderick sees me lying here? I can hardly tell him I'm on holiday in Scotland, can I?'

Smith, an expert on surveillance operations, finally gave the all clear and ordered that Adamson be brought to the control room in the hotel as quickly as possible. The detective was escorted at speed along the deep-carpeted corridors to the operation centre. Smith said: 'With the suspect now in the suite and talking to his uncle and aunt, there was an air of excitement amongst us. At first everyone was grabbing the earphones but after a while the interest faded. Roderick was talking about the family, in particular his granny, whom he had just seen, and his Falkland adventures. Everyone took off the earphones one by one with boredom, except for the technician who was monitoring the sound levels, changing the tapes and telling us what was going on. The sound was perfect, but all we had after one and a half hours was family chit-chat.' Jim Smith had installed advanced equipment for the sting and laid on his most experienced team all, so far, for a stream of family chatter.

But in the suite Stephen was in fact biding his time and luring Roderick into a sense of remorse. With his eye on the clock, and knowing that the tape in the sofa had only a two-hour span, he suggested a breath of fresh air. By strolling around the gardens, he had given the police an opportunity to change the old tape for a new one, which they hoped would contain a little more than just chit-chat.

All of a sudden it was there: the truth coming out. Everyone in the control room jumped into action, grabbing the earphones. They could not get enough of it. Just two doors away, as Desmond de Silva was to say, 'Roderick gazed into the face of his father's identical twin, there spilled from his lips the pent-up guilt that he had harboured for so long and which finally broke its banks in a series of admissions that point inescapably to the conclusion that he is responsible for patricide and matricide.'

In the next ninety minutes Roderick made what a leading forensic psychologist concluded was an entirely free and voluntary confession. Dr Gisli Gudjonsson has provided vital evidence in support of the successful appeals by the Guildford Four, the Birmingham Six and the Tottenham Three, but after listening to the tapes made at the Dunkeld Hotel, he said they made up one of the most convincing admissions to murder he had ever heard.

Often with tears in his eyes, fiddling with the collar of his open-neck shirt and toying with the buttons of his blazer, Roderick told his uncle that his parents' bodies had been wrapped in plastic and well camouflaged. Pushing him further, Stephen urged him to lead the police to the secret grave, so that they could at least have a decent Christian burial. Roderick admitted that he carried the blame, but gave a clear hint that Mark was involved too. He stressed there could be no mitigating circumstances for what he had done.

If the police moved in on him, he would have no hesitation in committing suicide, because he had no intention of sitting in a prison cell for twenty-five years. He also feared that the truth about the murders would kill his grandmother. In the middle of this traumatic scene there was a knock on the door and a maid brought in plates of scones, cakes and huge slices of strawberry tart. Stephen offered his nephew a plate as Gay poured the tea, but commented that the conversation was hardly the type to stimulate an appetite. But for two Jersey detectives who had not eaten since breakfast, the arrival of tea had certainly set their tummies rumbling.

As the conversation went on, Roderick started to cry his heart out, his words only coming out after long silences. Stephen and Gay remained silent while their nephew talked about the bodies being buried in the clothes they were wearing. If, Roderick said as the tapes rolled on, he had been a Catholic, he would have sought absolution. He also said he was looking forward to seeing his parents 'on the far side'.

Uncle Stephen: 'To say you are sorry?'

Roderick: 'No.'

Stephen suggested there would not be much evidence left on the bodies now, but Roderick said that the clothes they were still wearing would show scientists exactly on which night they were killed.

'I don't think I would mind too much paying the price,' he said, but added that he needed legal advice. He had, he told his uncle and aunt, to live alone with his guilt.

Desmond de Silva, in the Gibraltar extradition court, said that the tapes 'amount to the clearest confession to being involved in murder that a person could make, short of the use of the phrase "yes I did it".' The QC said that the Dunkeld House Hotel tapes, with Roderick's confession to Helena Pedo, 'together with certain established events and scientific discoveries at the scene of the killing and elsewhere in Jersey, amounts to a carefully planned and brutally executed double murder with infinite cunning being deployed in the disposal of the bodies . . . and elaborate steps taken to shield himself from the guilt which years later he confessed to'.

After five years, Detectives Marks and Adamson finally had the evidence which had eluded Jersey CID for so long, but the four-hour tapes still had to be transcribed, dissected and presented in a dossier before the legal authorities in the island could issue the arrest warrant.

Marks and Adamson could have taken a chance and seized Roderick as he walked out of the hotel, but the officers had noted carefully that Roderick had said he was going back to see Nan Clark in Fulham the following day, when they hoped he might indicate where the bodies were to be found. Giving Roderick that opportunity would also mean more time for Jersey's Attorney General Philip Bailhache to listen to the tapes and issue the warrant.

Smith, who was technically in charge of the Scottish end of the operation, supported the decision not to move in straight away. 'There was no power of arrest north of the border in this situation. The Jersey police were in close liaison with their Attorney General and he would not have wanted an immediate arrest. He wanted to be 100 per cent sure rather than make a pre-emptive strike.'

Roderick left the hotel at 7 p.m. As Emma-Jane's VW turned into the road at the bottom of the drive, some of the Scottish surveillance team were manoeuvring to shadow him. The two Jersey detectives were exhausted, but were quick to offer their grateful thanks to Jim Smith and his colleagues. Everyone left was invited to the local pub for a drink. But as soon as the islanders put their hands in their pockets, they didn't have the means to buy a round. They had not had time to change their Jersey notes and coins, currency not recognized in Scotland.

Said Smith, 'It was very funny. We Scotsmen are always described as being mean with our money, but this was a new trick to me: to offer a drink and then try and pay for it with funny money!'

Roderick was being tailed, but it was a hair-raising drive south. At times they were doing more than 100 m.p.h. as he weaved dangerously through the heavy traffic on the M6. To the Scottish police behind him, he appeared hyped-up, a man very much on the run or, as Maureen Ellam would say, on a high. He was stopping at service stations, popping from one telephone box to another as if frightened that his calls would be traced if he stayed too long on one line. With his military training, he sensed that he was being followed, and his erratic progress was partly to see who was behind him.

He called his grandmother in North Berwick and certainly Mark in Paris. Then, he called Nan Clark in

Fulham, telling her he would see her at 2 p.m. the following day, but what followed persuaded him not to keep that appointment. Instead, he decided to make a dash for freedom, to avoid the net that was fast closing in.

At yet another service station area near Warrington, he spotted the car he had been suspicious of for over 100 miles. At the next exit, junction 21, he gave police the slip.

'We were very disappointed, but there again he was a former soldier and knew all about evasion tactics. Even so, the operation had been a success and a first-class example of co-operation between forces a long way apart,' said Smith. 'I'm sure they did not anticipate having to come so far to get their man, or how quickly they would get help or co-operation. That is not always the case between individual police forces in this country; there is rivalry between some of them . . . and even within some forces.'

Detectives now had the evidence, but they had lost their man.

11

Los Angeles 6463624

Well pleased with himself for having shaken off the police tail by driving twice round a roundabout and taking a minor exit, Roderick was about to motor into the biggest murder manhunt in London for many years and, indeed, become a suspect. A dark blue Golf GTi was seen at Wimbledon Common around the time Rachel Nickell, a blonde model, was killed in a frenzy of stabbing in front of her toddler son as they walked their dog.

Roderick had parked the car outside Emma-Jane's flat in Holyport Road at four o'clock on the Wednesday morning. While he rested for a few hours to recover from that high-speed dash down from Scotland, Fulham police had staked out her old flat. By the time they recognized their error, Roderick was long gone.

'I returned from holiday that morning to find that Roderick had left a nice thank-you note and a bottle of whisky for me,' Emma-Jane recalled. 'Suddenly there was a thumping at the door and the police were on my doorstep. I was absolutely shattered. At first they thought he was something to do with the Rachel Nickell murder. I told them that the radiator grille on the car seemed to have been damaged while I was away but repaired. Next thing I know, the newspapers got very excited that the police were looking for him for killing his parents, which I had no idea about. My life was "interesting" for the next twenty-four hours, with the press camped on my doorstep and reporters shouting at me, asking if I was his girlfriend.

'I put it down to experience now, but all I was trying to do was to help him at the time. It seemed to me to be all very involved, but from my point of view it was so small. A day later the newspapers had forgotten all about it.'

The police had not forgotten, however, and continued to question her for some days. 'They kept coming back to see me, thinking I had some big secret. But I did not know anything. I hardly knew the guy. He stayed in my flat on his own while I was in Italy and I had no idea where he had gone,' she said.

Emma-Jane, an artist who has had her work exhibited, was at the time of the trial resting between jobs. She unknowingly echoed many of Donna Westend's feelings towards Roderick: 'People do not seem to understand him. They take a view that he must be evil to have done what he did. But they should try and understand why. I do not know the answer to that, but I do not think he should be condemned straight away.'

Detectives Marks and Adamson flew from Edinburgh to Heathrow and met Attorney General Philip Bailhache, who had arrived from Jersey. Mr Bailhache decided that he wanted to listen to the four hours of the tapes. What he heard was more than enough: he authorized a warrant for the arrest of Roderick Newall for the murders of his parents.

In anticipation, Adamson had prepared an affidavit detailing how the tapes were obtained and the witnesses to them. But where was their man? A description of Roderick was circulated to every police force in the country as well as Interpol. The hunt for Roderick was officially on.

Meanwhile, Adamson had a strange task to perform: to come to Roderick's aid. He told his colleagues at Fulham CID that Roderick had had nothing to do with the Wimbledon Common murder, which one national tabloid had put on its front page, but that he was wanted for the murder of his parents.

Roderick had once again disappeared, and the posse of detectives had no idea where he had gone. Paul Marks later explained the attempts to track him down. A marine agency, which claimed to have contacts in all marinas along the western European seaboard, was employed, but came up with nothing.

Police, who at first thought he might be involved in

drug running and was staying in Amsterdam, missed a remark on the tapes which revealed that he was planning to go to Southampton. This was exactly what he did. Within hours of arriving back in London from Scotland, he took a train from Waterloo and caught a ferry from the Hampshire port to France.

Nan Clark confirmed that she had received a call from him cancelling their 2 p.m. appointment. At the time, he was crossing the Channel, only to discover that there were problems with his new yacht the *Austral Soma*, which was taking on water. With a new crisis threatening Roderick, Mark had left his Paris banking office in a hurry for an emergency meeting with his brother in Boulogne. There he told Roderick in no uncertain terms to get far away, and as quickly as possible. Crewman Steve Beldham said later that there had been a terrible panic in the rush to get out of harbour and into the safety of the oceans.

With police in despair, one of the contacts they had built up during the long years of the investigation came good. Mark was coming to London on 29 July and had booked in at his favourite hotel: Blakes in South Kensington. Another covert operation was mounted, this time with the Metropolitan Police.

Blakes fitted Mark perfectly. Each of its sixty bedrooms and suites offered, as the hotel claims in its publicity, 'style and elegance to the travelled connoisseur and convenience and efficiency to the international businessman'. Owner Anouska Hempel designed the decor with antiques, paintings, rare silks and velvets, and she boasts, 'There is only one Blakes.'

Scotland Yard decided they wanted to photograph Mark to see if he had changed his appearance over the past few years. They phoned a department specializing in secret photography. They could have snapped him with a long lens at the airport and he would not have known, but they did it at the hotel, with a camera hidden in a specially adapted briefcase. When he was welcomed by the reception desk as a known and respected guest he failed to notice not only the man with the briefcase but the two plain-clothes detectives from the Met's Intelligence Squad.

He retired to his room, dialled room service and settled down to wait. At precisely 2 a.m. he dialled a fourteen-digit number. The officers made a note of it and the Metropolitan Police passed it on to Jersey.

'We did not know what the number was, so we dialled it as well,' said a detective.

DS Charles MacDowall dialled 010-1-310-646-36-24 and a female voice answered, 'Can I help you?'

'Yes – who are you?'

'This is Air France Reservations Desk in Los Angeles.'

After identifying himself, MacDowall was told that Mark had booked a morning flight from Heathrow to Paris, Paris to Madrid and on to Tangier. Mark had flown to London, picked up some papers from a Post Office box number, then phoned halfway across the world to set up his clandestine meeting with his brother.

Within a few hours, on Wednesday 29 July 1992, he had flown out of Heathrow, never to return to London again. As Mark flew south, Adamson was on the phone to the Royal Gibraltar Police, where he spoke to DI Louis Wink in the Rock's CID. Could he get someone over to Tangier quickly to check if the yacht *Austral Soma* was there and who was aboard it?

'That was tricky,' said Wink. Political relations between the colony and Morocco are always very delicate, so any surveillance would have to be carried out under cover. But he would try. Two drug squad officers, Albert Virgas and Isaac Messiah, were sent across as tourists. They found the yacht and then rented a room in a small hotel overlooking the harbour to keep observation.

Their orders were so strict, never to take their eyes off the boat, that if one was out of the building on a break the other dared not leave his post, even to go to the toilet. Several times, when left on his own, one of the officers refused to come and take phone calls, leaving the Rock's Police Headquarters frustratingly out of touch with developments.

On Saturday 1 August, the authorities in Jersey and the Ministry of Defence in London reached agreement to use the navy, if necessary, to track Roderick down. HMS *Ranger*, a fast patrol launch attached to Gibraltar Protection, and HMS *Argonaut*, a frigate with a glorious Falklands record, were put on standby.

On Monday 3 August, the two drug squad officers bribed a guard to get into the marina and, checking the boat, identified Roderick and one other man aboard. The following afternoon, it looked as if the *Austral Soma* was preparing to go to sea.

MacDowall, now in Gibraltar with Adamson, drew up the operation plan with the local police. Louis Wink would head the firearms unit of five officers, plus MacDowall to serve the warrant. At 8 p.m. the message came from Tangier that the yacht was under sail, heading south following the Moroccan coastline. In the operations room at Gibraltar Police HQ, hamburgers and Cokes had just been brought in. They were hastily abandoned as the officers rushed to the harbour to board HMS *Ranger* and set off in pursuit.

What was to follow would be unprecedented in the history of the Royal Navy.

12

Operation Snowball

Lieutenant Commander Tim Appleyard, skipper of HMS *Ranger*, was playing the organ in King's Chapel when his bleeper went off to summon him to report to the duty officer at the navy headquarters on Gibraltar. He was stunned by his orders to be on standby for immediate departure to hunt down and detain on the high seas a suspected murderer heading for the South Atlantic from Morocco.

Three days later, at 2015 hours he got a second bleep – this time an emergency 999 – and soon he was at full speed, heading through the Straits of Gibraltar and out into the Atlantic.

'By the time we got off Tangier it was dark and I started looking at my radar at all the blips, which we call contacts, trying to work out which was our man,' said Appleyard, renowned for his intimate local knowledge, which has led to a spate of successful rescue operations.

'Fifty per cent of my work is searching for vessels. So this was nothing special for me, although I have never helped in the arrest of a murder suspect at gunpoint. It was a process of elimination. We could ignore anyone coming into the Med, but once we got out into the Atlantic it was much busier and much more difficult.'

The *Ranger*, capable of twenty-two knots over a range of 550 miles, had aboard the Gibraltar firearms unit and its own ten crew that night. Slicing through a heavy swell and swirling currents where the Med and Atlantic meet at such a narrow neck is not the best place to find sea-legs. As Appleyard says, with the understated and slightly superior style of a mariner, 'I have to say that the police were not enjoying the trip very much. They were arming themselves, loading their magazines and at the same time stuffing anti-seasick tablets down their throats. To operate at sea is an acquired skill.'

Louis Wink, a tough and efficient policeman on land, was groaning at the ordeal. 'We were bobbing up and down like a cork in the water. It was a rough time for us and one that I will never forget. It is not every day that you go out on to the high seas to make an arrest, thank God!'

At 1 a.m. they sighted and identified the *Austral Soma*, no mean achievement in busy waters where freighters and tankers enter and leave the Atlantic in never-ending lanes of traffic, all amid fishing boats, pleasure craft, Moroccan gunboats and the odd high-speed vessel powered by huge outboard motors, making the dash to a lonely Spanish beach under cover of darkness, packed with hashish.

They closed in on their prey to confirm what they had seen in their night sight equipment, but the *Austral Soma* was still in Moroccan waters and safe from arrest. The rules of the unique operation had been spelt out clearly by legal and diplomatic experts at the Ministry of Defence and the Foreign Office in Whitehall. The *Austral Soma* could be intercepted and Newall detained only if she was flagless or flying the Red Ensign and sailing in international waters. Any breach of the regulations would jeopardize any hope of getting Newall back to Jersey legally to stand trial.

Throughout his run from France to escape the arrest warrant, Roderick had been extra-careful to keep well clear of British waters and Crown jurisdiction. That's why he met with Mark in Tangier; Britain has no extradition treaty with Morocco. *Ranger* had to ensure that it did not give Roderick any grounds to suspect that he was being followed, causing him to alter his course and hug the African coastline for safety.

As Wink recalled: 'We did a sweep past him, and as we neared him he shot his powerful searchlight over us. So we had to make him believe we were checking all the ships in the area, posing as a Moroccan patrol boat on fishery protection duty.'

Once the *Austral Soma* had been identified, the

Ranger pulled back five miles and waited for the frigate HMS *Argonaut* to arrive. The *Argonaut* commander, Captain Bob Stevens, was having dinner with his wife, his mother-in-law and Captain Stewart Tickner, the naval commander on the Rock, when he was ordered to put to sea.

'My attitude was that if Drake could finish his game of bowls then I could finish my meal,' he said. 'We were given eight hours' notice to put out and we did it in three and a half, which is pretty impressive for an old steam ship. But I always say: give sailors a tough task and they will respond. We were in Gibraltar at that time for maintenance and on standby to go to Bosnia. I had been alerted by special signal some days earlier that we might be needed to go out and arrest Newall, so we were on reduced notice and half expecting it when it came.

'I had spoken to the crew before we docked and told them whatever happens I would like them to take a responsible approach while ashore. I did not want to hear about any of my men being thrown through bar windows. I was not disappointed, because I sensed they thought it was going to be an adventure with a difference. The crew had a good night in the pubs and nobody was drunk.'

The *Argonaut*, armed with Exocet and Seacat missiles, anti-submarine torpedoes and a Lynx helicopter, was a veteran of the Falklands campaign, where it had been hit twice by Argentine bombs which entered the ship but did not explode. With that kind of war experience and firepower, it seemed a particularly large sledgehammer to crack the Newall nut. But the frigate was the only ship available, and Captain Stevens was treating the task as a deadly serious operation. He was to take no chances.

The *Argonaut* left bow waves as she steamed through the Straits at twenty-six knots, 'which was quite exciting', said Captain Stevens, and they met up with *Ranger* at 5 a.m. on 5 August 1992. DS Charles MacDowall, Wink and his men transferred to the warship to plan the tactics of the arrest.

Said Captain Stevens, 'I was concerned that Newall might have heavy-calibre weapons on board and that he might use them. I did not fancy the idea of writing to Mrs Bloggs or whoever telling her I had not taken sufficient precautions and that her son had been seriously injured or even killed. I was concerned about the difficulty of getting him out of his boat and on to mine without violence or threat to my chaps. I was very keen to go for the covert approach.'

By now the *Austral Soma* was out of Moroccan waters, and so the *Argonaut* moved in. With the crew at battle stations, the police firearms team, weapons ready and wearing flak jackets, hid at the back of the frigate on the helicopter landing bay. The ruse was to lure Roderick aboard by posing as a warship on exercise, to get him to row across to present his documents for a routine security check, but at first

Roderick refused to respond to the frigate's hooter.

Then Captain Stevens tried radio contact, informing the yacht: 'I am authorized to ask you to stop the vessel and the master, with proof of ID and the ship's papers, to transfer to us in your rowboat and report as necessary. You are to embark using my jumping ladder, port side aft. Regret that our boat was damaged by flotsam yesterday during another routine investigation.'

There was still no response from the *Austral Soma*, and both police and seamen were, as Wink said, becoming a little restless. 'If this was going to be a stand-off, the only other option would be to intercept, and we really did not want to do that. We would have to seek higher authority for what would probably have been an armed confrontation,' said the captain. 'Eventually, after more hooting and further calls over the radio, a voice answered and identified himself as Roderick Newall. He fell for our story, and jokingly said,"I will come on board, but you will have to offer me a cup of tea."'

'Certainly,' agreed Captain Stevens, 'we will have a nice cup ready for you.'

As Roderick rowed over, weapons were cocked. Roderick, dressed in cut-off shorts and a baggy red tee-shirt which officers noted could have concealed a gun, rowed across to the warship. He was met by a boarding officer in a flak jacket, who escorted him across the flight deck.

With a smile, the officer turned to Roderick and said quietly, 'We have got a surprise for you, old boy.' As he turned the corner, Roderick suddenly found six weapons pointing at his head. So stunned was he that at first he refused the order to spreadeagle himself on the deck until the police forced him down. He was handcuffed, searched and then MacDowall stepped forward to do what Jersey police had been waiting six long years to do: read the arrest warrant to him.

'He was very surprised, but he had that icy look we were to get to know so well. He looked at every weapon that was being pointed at him,' said Wink.

Roderick later told MacDowall that he had been assessing the exact weaponry ranged at him, working out how many people he could take out if he had a chance to grab one before being shot dead. He was also to say that had he known what was in store for him, he would have rammed his steel-hulled boat into the *Argonaut* at full speed. Captain Stevens confirmed that the *Austral Soma* was capable of holing his warship.

Roderick was frogmarched below deck as his crewman Steve Beldham was ordered to come aboard the *Argonaut*. Said Wink, 'We boarded the *Austral Soma* uncertain as to whether Mark Newall was there or not. The boat was very well equipped, clean and well kept. From the charts it appears they were heading initially for Brazil, from where there is no extradition to Jersey.'

On the *Argonaut* Roderick was fuming, shouting at

his armed guards. The police remembered that not only was he a highly-trained soldier suspected of killing two members of his own family, but that he had told his uncle on the taped confession that he would have no hesitation in committing suicide if arrested.

'Our problem was that we did not have a cell, and there were objects in the room where he was being held which could become weapons,' said Wink. 'So we sat him down handcuffed to a banister, with an armed officer watching him all the time. We gave him coffee and a blanket and talked freely with him. Formal questioning would start later.'

From this point, 160 miles south-west of Gibraltar, *Argonaut* altered course to steam back to the Rock with their quarry. A small party was put aboard the *Austral Soma*, including a scene-of-crime officer to bring it back, escorted by *Ranger*, to Gibraltar. Roderick was still taking drugs: cannabis was found hidden in the engine room.

That night, as the *Argonaut* docked, waiting on the quayside was Adamson with Captain Stevens's wife and family to welcome them. 'It had all been very exciting. I must admit the story of how we arrested a dangerous criminal at sea comes up often at dinner parties, and my mother-in-law, who is a New Zealander, seems to live off it all the time,' said the proud captain. 'In my twenty-seven years in the navy I have never had to do this kind of thing before.'

Captain Stevens was to underline this point in his

official report to the Admiralty. 'Operation Snowball was an unqualified success. The co-operation between the various police agencies and navy units which participated was unprecedented, and the final outcome a tribute to the professionalism of all concerned.'

13

A Medieval Dungeon

It was 2 a.m. in the Deputy Commissioner's office at Gibraltar's Police Headquarters when Adamson confronted the new prisoner for the first time. It started with a handshake. Adamson and MacDowall told Roderick to sit down. Roderick stared straight through the officers. He just sat there in silence and asked to speak to his lawyer in Jersey, David Le Quesne. He said that he would remain silent until his lawyer arrived.

As he was led away to his cell, Roderick turned to the two detectives and said that when David arrived he would be looking for a quick route back to Jersey. He repeated his intention to have the matter dealt with quickly and with as little hurt as possible for his family. However sincere he had been at this time in his desire to protect the feelings of his family, he very quickly decided that his best course was to fight extradition all the way.

An hour later, Roderick was remanded by magistrate Felix Pizzarello to Gibraltar's grim thirteenth-century Moorish castle prison for a week. The colonial-style courthouse on Main Street stands at the end of a twenty-yard pathway shaded by olive branches. On one side is the magistrate's court, where Mr Pizzarello dispenses justice on the minor and the trivial, or remands defendants for trial at higher courts. Opposite, is the grander Supreme Court with its polished woodwork decor, where the judges sit. The old building has a run-down, tatty look about it.

Here, one of the most dramatic hearings since the war took place: the inquest, in 1988, into the shooting by the SAS of three IRA terrorists planning a bombing attack on a British army parade. Now, Roderick was going to be the centre of another major legal battle attracting vast media attention. The link between the two cases was Gibraltar's most famous criminal lawyer, Christopher Finch.

Mr Finch had represented the families of the three dead terrorists and also the inquest's most famous witness, the striking Carmen Proetta, when she took Fleet Street for a small fortune in libel payments for attempting to discredit her as a witness. The robust lawyer with an ostentatious style, both inside court and outside, favoured chunky gold jewellery, and drove an immaculately kept Jaguar and a Rolls-Royce.

Any prisoner in the Moorish castle will greet incomers with the advice: 'Get Finch.' Even his main courtroom rivals in the Newall case paid due respect to both his ability and charisma. Desmond de Silva QC, no mean courtroom performer himself, said, 'He is known for his passionate oratory on behalf of his clients, and he proved himself to be a master of court procedures, which enabled him not only to prevent the extradition of Roderick for so long, but also came very close to having his client discharged on legal grounds.'

Gibraltar's Attorney General, John Blackburn Gittings, added, 'I suppose most people in the world who get arrested 160 miles south-west of Gibraltar have the name of Chris Finch on their lips. If they are in trouble, they want him. His reputation is that well known.'

Neither Roderick nor Finch had heard of each other before arriving in the old courthouse. But within twenty minutes, the lawyer was on the case. Blackburn Gittings, himself a renowned criminal lawyer in London before moving to the more peaceful atmosphere of Gibraltar, was in the town centre taking his mother to dinner when he heard about the arrest. One comment made that night was to stick in his mind. 'Felix Pizzarello told me: "I do not like the sound of this; it sounds like kidnapping!" I think that coloured his attitude, perhaps,' said the Attorney General.

The *Austral Soma* had been brought into Gibraltar's harbour and was scoured by police search teams. They found hard evidence that Roderick, instead of trying to forget the past, carried on board a blue suitcase full of family photographs. And crewmate Beldham explained that the reason Roderick had taken so long to answer the *Argonaut*'s radio messages was that he was hiding seventeen grammes of cannabis in the engine compartment.

Finch soon got to work with his books on law and the Gibraltar constitution. He complained about the means of arrest and the 'inhuman' prison conditions Roderick was enduring in the Moorish castle. He made bail applications and demanded a news blackout on court proceedings. Said Blackburn Gittings, 'My feeling at first was that it would be straightforward, with no real fuss. I had no idea then that it would ever go to the extent it did: all the way to the Appeal Courts – this was totally exceptional.'

Finch threatened to demand that Uncle Stephen and his wife be brought to Gibraltar for cross-examination on the confession tape.

After just one month in the Moorish castle, where even Louis Wink admitted that his officers guarding Roderick erected a tent to keep him warm, Roderick made the first of four attempts either to commit suicide or harm himself so badly as to get him into hospital. Whatever he intended, he very nearly killed himself. Roderick managed to get hold of a used razor blade. Under the cover of his blankets, he slashed both wrists and gouged his groin, in an apparent attempt to sever his femoral artery. He lay in his bed, his face covered, almost unconscious, with his life slipping away. A guard, convinced that the prisoner was fast asleep, was about to close the spyhole when he noticed that Roderick's left hand had slipped from the bed and was dripping blood on to the floor.

Said Blackburn Gittings, 'Another two minutes and it would have been too late. But I still don't know if it was a *cri-de-coeur* or a real attempt. A professional soldier would know how to do it. He must have known what to do. I had a lot of strong letters from Chris Finch, but conditions were no worse there than for anybody else. I think it is a fairly soft regime compared with London prisons.'

One Gibraltar policeman also doubted the suicide bid. 'He knew the times of the routine checks and this happened just before one of them. But there is no doubt that it could have been fatal.'

Roderick was soon on his way to a full recovery after treatment in the intensive care unit at the Rock's St Bernard's Hospital, only to find out a week later that he would have to wait another fifty-five days in the prison, which he described as hell, for the full extradition hearing to begin.

The prison governor, Superintendent Emilio Enriles, in his first and only comment about the Newall case, insisted that Roderick 'suffered no less deprivation of basic human rights and comforts than any other remand prisoner loses by virtue of his imprisonment – however his unstable behaviour led to a need for strict controls and supervision'.

Far from being singled out, the governor claims, Roderick was better off than other prisoners. 'His cell was no different to any of those in the main detention area in terms of size, lighting, ventilation and fittings. But in terms of heating he was better off than others, as his cell was the only one fitted with a fan heater.'

Yet there is much to support Roderick's claims that he was being held in inhuman conditions. The prison was condemned in a recent official report as being a 'medieval dungeon' and local politicians agreed that a new gaol is urgently needed, but acknowledge there is no money to build one.

Governor Enriles, however, defends his prison as being well up to modern European standards: 'It may lack certain facilities which are available at prisons in larger countries, but the castle does not trail behind in standards,' he said. 'On key issues such as treatment, rehabilitation and care for the prisoner, our standards are significantly high and, without a shadow of a doubt, we take pride in the way we treat our inmates.'

Roderick showed that he was totally unimpressed by such claims, and he started a hunger strike in protest, which lasted only a few days. Fears started to mount at the highest level that a plot existed for either a prison breakout or of an attempt to snatch him from custody. Security was suddenly stepped up to an unprecedented level after a phone call to Roderick was monitored. No details were given, but by November every court appearance was a show of force.

Six plain-clothes officers, including members of Gibraltar's Special Branch armed with semi-automatic weapons, escorted Roderick on the ten-minute drive from the prison to court in a four-vehicle cavalcade with lights flashing and sirens wailing, clearing a way through the packed streets to the courthouse. Barbed wire had been erected around the courtyard at the back of the building for the first time in living memory. In Magistrate Pizzarello's courtroom, officers flanked Roderick as he sat in his now customary court-appearance clothes of a white open-necked shirt, jeans and blue blazer, hunched forward listening to Finch giving the Crown a hard time.

As questions mounted about the open display of firearms and security, costing some £2,000 a day, a prison official revealed that the alert was sparked by a phone call from an unknown British woman, who said to Roderick, 'Do not worry if things go wrong. We can sort it out. There are people working for you.'

When questioned by Rock detectives, Roderick said that he vaguely remembered the phone call but could not give them any details. It was the start of many strange goings on on the Rock over the coming years.

Wink was to reveal: 'Roderick was the highest-security inmate at the prison. We were worried what he might do, not only because he was a highly trained soldier, but quite clearly he also had moments of deep depression. We received a flow of intelligence from Jersey which pointed to the possibility that he might attempt to escape, either through his own means or with assistance from outside.

'It drained our resources to guard him. Our elite squad of firearm officers was entirely tied up with him. Experience showed us that whenever the case turned against him, tension would build up and we had to be at our most alert.'

Governor Enriles said that all of Roderick's letters, phone calls and visits – except those from his lawyers – were monitored in line with prison regulations. But he accepted that breaches of security were almost inevitable: 'Penal establishments all over the world have problems of trafficking of illicit and unauthorized articles. As prison governors, we have controls and measures, but the reality is that some filter through. It is unfair to single out the castle as being any more lax than others.'

Roderick's years at public school and in the army had prepared him well for the regime of prison life. The governor and staff remember him as being 'respectful, well educated and courteous'. His manners deserted him only when his requests were turned down, when he would become unco-operative and withdrawn. But he never threatened violence against any of the staff.

'His daily routine was the same as any other remand prisoner. In the morning he would clean and tidy his wing and perform other tasks allotted him. After that, he had access to the gym, television, books, newspapers and board games,' said the governor. 'Roderick was particularly keen on challenging staff and fellow prisoners to a game of chess.'

The prison kitchen also did its best to fit in with the requirements of the milk-products-based vegetarian diet Roderick had taken up since his days in New Zealand. The governor says, 'Roderick got on well with his fellow prisoners, British and foreign alike, and was angry when he was put in isolation for security reasons.'

There were also security fears back in Britain. Alistair Clark asked for extra security for his wife at their Fulham home, and local police later confirmed that a panic-alarm button was installed. Nan Clark reported that Mark had been on the phone to her.

Stephen Newall, at his home in Rhu in Scotland, had also informed police that Mark had telephoned from Paris, trying to pressure him into withdrawing his evidence against Roderick. 'How many people have to die?' Mark had pleaded with his uncle, indicating that Roderick was going through hell in Gibraltar prison and was threatening another suicide attempt. Gay had listened in to Mark's call on an extension in the next room, and had written it down almost word for word. Dumbarton CID stepped up patrols in the neighbourhood and also installed a security alarm.

However, Mark denied making any threats to the family when Jersey police contacted him in Paris demanding an explanation.

The legal showdown over Finch's application that the taped confession be ruled inadmissible, thus making extradition impossible, was booked for Mr Pizzarello's court on 19 November 1992. The press arrived on the Rock en masse, giving the Rock's Holiday Inn its biggest boost to trade since the IRA/SAS inquest. Some of the reporters amused themselves before court started by bellowing at Roderick as he was brought out of prison, 'Where's the bodies, Roddy?'

The Crown had drafted in a top legal gun in the substantial form of Desmond de Silva, a name respected not only in the English courts, but around the Commonwealth. Although starting as a defender, his services had been more lately sought by the Crown in complex trials abroad including treason, in which the prosecution sought the death penalty. Well over six feet tall, de Silva, with his flamboyant turn of phrase and colourful courtroom presence, made an intriguing contrast with Christopher Finch. Their battle royal across the bar was keenly anticipated by press and lawyers alike.

De Silva, a City of London Councillor who is married to the Queen's niece Princess Katarina of Yugoslavia, is no snob. He is equally comfortable with policemen, lawyers and journalists, all of whom he invariably addresses as 'dear boy'. He delights in reminding friends and colleagues that the *Daily Telegraph* once bestowed on him the nickname 'The Scarlet Pimpernel of the Bar'.

The Crown counsel was selected from a list of six names of London QCs by the Jersey Attorney General Philip Bailhache to tackle the unique circumstances of the case of a man being arrested in international waters by police aboard a British warship. And he was about to walk into a major setback, one that left Roderick 'cock-a-hoop' in the words of Blackburn Gittings.

When Pizzarello called the court to order, dozens of pressmen were furious to find that he had allowed Finch's application for the hearing to be held in camera. Despite Blackburn Gittings's appeal that the decision smacked of 'justice behind closed doors', the press were left standing outside court in the late-autumn Gibraltar sunshine while the vital tape and its contents were discussed.

Blackburn Gittings had listened to the tape weeks before, and was, as a result, convinced of Roderick's guilt: 'I thought it was a cert after I heard the tapes. I sat down for four hours one Sunday morning and switched them on.' Gibraltar's Attorney General added, 'I was very depressed when I listened to them; I have done lots of murders – babies boiled alive and children pushed up chimneys – but I was very moved by what Roderick said to his uncle.'

But Magistrate Pizzarello had a far different interpretation. At 4 p.m. on Friday, 20 November, the press were called back into court to hear him read his seven-page judgment, scrawled in his spidery handwriting full of crossings out and corrections. The gallery strained to catch his words in the appalling acoustics of the magistrate's court.

The cricket-loving magistrate, an important part of the Rock's establishment, ruled that the police had acted in a 'sneaky' way in obtaining the confession and ruled that it was unfair to Roderick. 'It was brought into being by the calculated attempt of the police through the agency of persons who could lull the defendant into a false sense of security,' he said. 'I do not believe the police acted improperly in the investigative sense but it is clearly improper in the forensic sense. For they used an avenue in a sneaky way of circumventing the right to silence.'

He praised the courage of Stephen and Gay Newall in speaking to Roderick about the murders, but said that he would have liked to have heard them give evidence in person. 'The tape recordings are in the nature of a confession, but in the exercise of discretion and in the circumstances of this case I disallow them.'

The court was in uproar. For the first time in months, Roderick grinned broadly as he was led from court and shouted 'No' to the yells from reporters asking for his reaction. As Roderick was being escorted back to his castle dungeon, to await the court's final decision the next Wednesday, Finch with an air of barely suppressed triumph held court to a pack of reporters.

'The Crown will now have to reconsider its position, and the case could be terminated by

MISSING PERSONS

HAVE YOU SEEN
THESE PEOPLE?

NICHOLAS NEWALL
56 Yrs — 5′ 11″ Tall
ack/Grey Hair — Broad Build
Dark Complexion

ELIZABETH NEWALL
47 Yrs — 5′ 10″ Tall
Light Red Hair —
Freckled Complexion
Scars on Back of Hands

**MR. & MRS. NEWALL WERE LAST SEEN ON OR AROUND
SUNDAY 11TH OCTOBER 1987**

HE POLICE ARE MOST ANXIOUS TO TRACE THESE PEOPLE
— AND ARE CONCERNED FOR THEIR SAFETY —

TELEPHONE THE INCIDENT ROOM **72240**
OF POLICE H.Q. **75511**

all started as a missing persons inquiry – the police poster
istributed throughout Jersey.

Above: Nicholas Newall.
Opposite: Elizabeth Newall.

Top: The Crow's Nest, overlooking the secret burial sites.
Below: The Newalls' Spanish villa.
Below right: Nicholas aboard the Chanson de Lecq.

Top: Desmond de Silva QC (in hat) and senior police officers during the search for the bodies at Grève de Lecq.

Bottom: The bodies are found and police erect sheeting to protect the grave.

op: Roderick Newall.
low: Mark Newall.

Roderick on his way to court under the armed escort of the Gibraltar police.

Wednesday,' he told them. 'In my personal opinion, I think they should do the honourable thing, as the magistrate has ruled against them, and drop all charges against my client.'

Told of Finch's comment, a furious Desmond de Silva boomed, 'That's his view; we will have to wait and see.' He admitted later: 'The Crown's case was in tatters at that moment, and we knew that the defence was getting ready to issue a press statement upon Roderick's anticipated release on Wednesday.' On the magistrate's ruling he growled in fury, 'Sneaky! I have never heard that word used since I was at prep school.' Sitting outside on the terrace of the Holiday Inn among white-faced and horrified detectives and lawyers, he was to boom, 'We have four days to get this case back on the rails.'

With the press completely unaware, the QC called a 2 a.m. meeting in his penthouse suite, attended by his entire team of lawyers and detectives. Then he issued the order to go and get Helena Pedo.

A jubilant Finch flew to London that night, reflecting on a week in which he had successfully defended Carmen Proetta against a drugs charge and now appeared to be on the brink of winning an astonishing victory which would secure Roderick his freedom. He was asked by one of the authors, jokingly, if he intended to raise his fees. 'Put them up?' he replied with a smile. 'If I did that, the only person who could afford me would be the Queen of Sheba!'

14

A Brazilian Beauty

Jersey detectives had not wanted to produce Helena
Pedo's evidence at the extradition hearing, but now
the Crown was forced to play the ace up its sleeve. If
only they could persuade her to come to Jersey to
swear a statement!

They had found Pedo's name among many others
in Roderick's filofax aboard the *Austral Soma*. As soon
as Finch had demanded the return of the diary, police
knew it contained something important that Roderick
wanted hidden. The detectives back in Jersey tried to
trace Helena. Roderick had written his most personal
phone numbers in code with all the digits mixed up. It
took weeks of constant dialling and redialling before
they suddenly hit on the right number. Astonishingly,
Helena picked up the phone and said, 'I've been
waiting a year to tell you this. It has been preying on
my mind.'

Adamson's gentle, reassuring Scots burr slowly put

her at ease. Then, over the transatlantic connections, she gave details of the mental anguish she had been suffering. 'I first became friendly with Roderick when I saw him walking into the Yacht Club at the marina here in Pôrto Alegre, and I got to know him well over the coming months,' she said. 'He later told me that he had killed his parents. I asked him what he had done with the bodies but he would not tell me.'

The detective had tracked her down six weeks after Roderick's arrest. Helena said that she was frightened because of what Roderick had done and that she feared for her life if she came forward to give evidence against him. For three weeks, Marks and Adamson tried to persuade her to change her mind, but she was adamant. On 11 October, they realized they were going to have to fly to Brazil, both to reassure her and persuade her to make a statement, so on 12 October they flew to South America, arriving in São Paulo in the early hours the following morning, where the driver for the British Consulate in the city took them to a downtown hotel.

Despite his patrol days in the tough areas of Glasgow, Adamson as well as Marks felt intimidated by the teeming city after the peace of Jersey. To them there seemed to be guns everywhere, even armed guards at the British Consulate despite the good diplomatic relations between Britain and Brazil.

The next day, the officers made contact with Helena. She said bluntly that she could not see them at all, because she was frightened for her own family's safety. The officers told her not to worry, that they were getting the next flight to Pôrto Alegre to see her.

They were met at the resort's airport by the British Honorary Consul Jeff Powell, who took them to the Grand Hotel near the beach front. After a great deal of persuasion, Helena agreed to come to the hotel that evening. To their immense relief she came – a willowy, dark-haired woman, described by Desmond de Silva as a 'young Brazilian beauty'. She was clearly frightened, faced with the prospect of talking to two British detectives in a country where there was little respect for police and even less for an informant.

Helena said that the persuasive powers of Adamson and Marks gave her confidence, and she agreed to return the following day to give them a full statement. By midday, the detectives had the evidence they had travelled so many miles to get. Helena even added details given to her by Roderick about how and why he had killed his parents. She pointed to a bottle of whisky on the table and explained that Roderick had blamed heavy drinking on the fateful night in October 1987 for causing 'a banging noise in his head'. All these years later, he told her, he bitterly regretted what he had done.

Helena gave the officers letters that Roderick had written to her, but made them promise that only a select handful of people should be made aware of what she had said. The detectives concocted a false story to prevent any hint of Helena's co-operation leaking out. They returned to the island insisting that they had failed to persuade her to speak, that they had brought back no new evidence. That the CID chief and his main investigator on the case thought it fit that other colleagues should be kept in the dark emphasized a fast-emerging new factor in the murders.

Not only was Helena Pedo worried about her safety; close relatives of the suspects were, too. It had become obvious in Gibraltar that the witnesses were in real danger, particularly if they were going to have to give evidence in court. Roderick's Brazilian lover was going to be given, within a few weeks, as much protection as the Jersey authorities could manage, but just one month after giving the commitment of discretion to Helena, the ruling by Gibraltar Magistrate Feliz Pizzarello, throwing out Roderick's taped confession in the Dunkeld Hotel, created a whole new situation.

As the Crown lodged an appeal against the ruling in a desperate bid to gain themselves more time, Helena had now to be persuaded to come to Jersey to swear her statement in front of the island's Bailiff, so it could be used in the extradition.

Desmond de Silva and his team were aware that Finch had demanded that Roderick's passport be brought back from Jersey to Gibraltar so that his client, who, he was confident, would be freed within a few days, could leave the colony aboard his yacht and escape the police, probably for ever. De Silva, displaying his normal air of confidence when repeating his rallying cry of 'getting the case back on the rails', was in fact a worried man. That weekend, late in November 1992, he confessed: 'Frankly, we are near to losing Roderick. If we don't win the next round, we are sunk. I cannot see how we can prevent him being given his freedom otherwise.'

Ian Christmas, the legal adviser to the Jersey police, was now almost permanently in Gibraltar and de Silva's right-hand man spent hours on the telephone to the island's Attorney General Philip Bailhache. Alarm bells were ringing everywhere. Gibraltar and Jersey detectives tried to ascertain whether they could rearrest Roderick as he took his first steps of freedom through the court's garden and down to his yacht at the marina. Could he be held for possessing the seventeen grammes of cannabis they had found aboard the *Austral Soma*?

In reality, they had nothing on him without the taped confession, and the haven of Tangier was just a few miles away.

That weekend, one of Roderick's cronies from the Falklands turned up at the Holiday Inn. He was as surprised to see Jersey detectives staying with the legal team as they were to see him. He claimed that he was only on holiday on the adjoining Costa del Sol, but later cheerfully admitted he had come to help Roderick make his speedy exit from the Rock.

Across Britain, news editors in television, radio and newspapers sent their teams to the Rock to get Roderick's first words as he was released. The tabloids prepared their chequebooks for what they expected to be a hard-fought battle to win his exclusive story.

At the Moorish castle, perched high on the imposing Rock from where he could see both the Moroccan coast and his yacht in the harbour complex, Roderick bragged to his guards: 'I'm being released on Wednesday; my lawyer has assured me I will be out on Wednesday.' But while Roderick was confident he would soon be at sea again, legal experts on extradition were poring over their books in the Temple next to the Royal Courts of Justice in London, searching for ammunition. Finally, they came to the conclusion that Pizzarello did not have the right of a trial judge in deciding what evidence was admissible. In their learned opinion, the magistrate's task was only to decide whether there was prima facie evidence to grant extradition.

The Crown team in Gibraltar worked late into the night, preparing their case for a judicial review, in layman's terms a demand that the Supreme Court overrule Pizzarello's ruling. But even if their application was successful, there was the serious fear that Roderick would be granted bail and run for it – that was obvious from his phone calls from prison.

Lawyers striding the 150 yards to court from the Holiday Inn and from Finch's chambers in the same square became an everyday sight. The Rock's Chief Justice, Alastair Kneller, set aside three days in late December for the Crown's appeal to be heard. That decision, holding up the case for a month, sent Finch into a furious attack when both sides met in the magistrate's court on the bail application two days later. He accused the Crown of going to the Chief Justice, 'sneaking in like thieves in the night while I was away from Gibraltar'. De Silva submitted that all proceedings, including the application for bail, should be 'frozen' until the appeal over the tapes had been heard. 'Nothing has changed. We still have strong reasons to believe that Newall will abscond if granted bail,' he said.

It was close, but the Crown won its breathing space. Now they needed Helena. In London, Adamson dialled her number, knowing just how much rested on this phone call. He spent more than an hour convincing her that she had to fly to Britain to ensure Roderick remained behind bars to face justice.

Helena admitted she agreed only after considerable doubt, but when the detective rang her back two days later to finalize the travel arrangements, she was still in great fear for her safety. Adamson promised the police would do everything to protect her and her family. To reassure her further they agreed that her close friend Eloisa Endres should be at her side throughout the whole trip.

Helena said she would be on the British Airways

flight from São Paulo to Heathrow, arriving on 2 December 1992. Marks and Adamson booked into the Tower Hotel overlooking Tower Bridge and St Catherine's Dock, where Roderick had bought the *Austral Soma* in June that year.

At 7 a.m. on 2 December, the two detectives, granted permission by airport security to meet the women airside, whisked them away with the minimum of fuss, straight to the hotel. The whole operation was intended to be carried out in total secrecy. It was imperative that the press did not get wind of Helena's presence in London, as any reports would tip off 'other interested parties' – the euphemistic expression used in Gibraltar, where the fear factor was at its highest.

Yet when the officers and the women sat down to breakfast next morning, there at the next table was the familiar face of Britain's most famous investigative reporter, Roger Cook.

'Oh Christ, look who it is,' the detectives thought. But Cook, thankfully, showed not the slightest interest in the four sitting close by. It later emerged that he had been at an awards dinner the night before and, having no involvement in the case, had no reason to recognize them. But it was a nasty moment.

On Friday 4 December, Helena and her friend were ushered into Jersey under the same cloak of secrecy, travelling as winter tourists. But the names on their tickets were false, and they travelled on flights separate from the detectives. At the island's small airport they were met by plain-clothes officers and driven to the island's court. The whole business took less than two hours, before the key witness and her friend were on the plane back to London.

London had relaxed the English teacher and her friend so much that they wished to stay on. They liked the all-expenses-paid lifestyle of a luxury hotel next to one of the world's most famous landmarks, the consideration of the officers and the security London offered them. But even when the detectives finally packed them on to their plane home, their safety was paramount. For within ten days, Helena's identity would have to be exposed in a Gibraltar court.

Adamson and Marks had the crucial statement documented correctly so it could be officially introduced as evidence in the extradition case, but when they flew back to Gibraltar a week later, they landed straight into the middle of a new crisis over Helena. De Silva had received information from a source which he has consistently refused to identify which suggested to him that Helena Pedo would never be in a position to give evidence. The Crown knew there could be only one interpretation of that: Helena was on a hit list and could end up as yet another victim of unexplained violence in Brazil. Lawyers have confirmed that an emergency meeting in Gibraltar over her immediate safety carried on well into the night of Tuesday 15 December.

She was urgently contacted by phone and warned of her potential danger. Within twenty-four hours, Helena and her family were moved out of their home and taken to a secret address. At the meeting, the possibility of armed guards for her was raised, but rejected because it would attract attention. Relocation was considered easier and more effective. Moves to Britain or the United States were mooted, but it was decided that immigration problems would be too complicated.

Jersey CID Chief Marks, a former Special Branch officer, and Adamson were the only two people ever to know where the witness and her family were living.

The *Jersey Evening Post* on 18 December 1992 splashed the news that Helena had been brought to the island in secret after she had been named by de Silva in the Gibraltar court that day. In a battle of wits with the defence, he had introduced the name of his new witness before Finch could object. He then made sure that the press reporters had the right spelling in their notebooks.

Back on the island, DI Martin Fitzgerald released a short statement stressing the security of Helena: 'We are not prepared to release any further information and no details relating to the operational aspect of this part of the inquiry will be made public.'

On St Valentine's Day 1993, Marks and Adamson, concerned about Helena's mounting fears for her safety, flew again to Brazil. In a resort in southern

Brazil, the detectives met up with Helena and her friend Eloisa. They told them to keep in close touch, not only with Jersey, but also with the local authorities.

From her secret address, Helena sat tight and waited for the drama in Gibraltar to unfold. 'My greatest fear was that Roderick might be set free at any moment and would head back to Brazil knowing what I had told the police,' she said later that year. 'He is a very dangerous person, and has to be locked up so he cannot harm anyone else.'

When she was told that Roderick was finally back in Jersey and had pleaded guilty to double murder, her reaction was: 'Thank God, I can feel safe again.'

15

Dirty Tricks

The threat to Helena Pedo was only one part of a dirty-tricks campaign, waged against the authorities and their witnesses, which was to send the prosecution and detectives almost into paranoia. There were accusations of phone tapping, and breaking into hotel rooms, and suspicions of a plot either to spring Roderick or silence him and his confession for ever. Even Finch believed his phone conversations were being monitored and angrily claimed to a prosecution lawyer that the Crown was responsible.

As the accusations from both sides built up, Roderick, by now the most guarded prisoner in the history of Gibraltar, somehow managed to make another suicide bid two days before Christmas, 1992. Although dressed only in shorts in midwinter, under a twenty-four-hours-a-day guard and with the lights in his cell never switched off, he managed to secrete a large amount of drugs and medication. Guards found him unconscious on his cell bed and he was to remain in a coma for nearly three days before staff at the intensive care unit of St Bernard's Hospital managed to pull him round.

Police refused to throw any light on the mystery as to how he had managed to make a second attempt on his life in less than three months. Later, it became obvious that the grim old fortress had its leaks.

This event only added to the general feeling of unease which was to last throughout the fifteen months Roderick was held in the colony. The authors were to learn that the reason for the clampdown on the prison after Christmas and the even tighter security every time Roderick was taken to court followed another phone call to the accused. He was apparently told: 'We have the best shots on the Rock and more are on the way. Money is no object.'

Detectives were convinced that the message was a broad hint to Roderick that a plan was being worked out to snatch him from prison or waylay the police as they brought the prisoner to court. Rumours were rife of a well-paid squad of criminals being formed to get Roderick off the rock. The Royal Gibraltar Police Force were taking no chances.

The days that were to follow in the high-ceilinged Supreme Court showed just how seriously the authorities were treating that message. Two armed officers from the Rock's elite firearms unit sat at corners of the upstairs gallery, cleared of the public at every hearing, their eyes scanning the movement below. They were relieved every half-hour. Other members of the unit with radio mikes and receivers guarded the main entrance and the rear of the building.

Detectives saw the comment that 'money was no object' as proof that the whole legal proceedings could be terminated. One Jersey officer said: 'I fear the only way we are going to get Roderick back is in a box.' It was well known that the whole Newall murder case would be finished if Roderick succeeded in one of his suicide attempts, yet despite being subjected to intense security someone was still able to slip him, yet again, the means to kill himself.

On 12 March 1993 an orange was passed to him in his cell. Inside was a syringe containing a drugs overdose. Once again Roderick was found unconscious and rushed back to St Bernard's. This time he was kept under observation for twelve hours and police started to probe how the security shield had been punctured yet again.

Finch was now using almost every remand appearance to protest against what he called 'the inhumane treatment and atrocious conditions' to which Roderick was being subjected. As the legal wrangle over the extradition continued, the lawyer said on 3 June 1993, 'Newall has never been treated as a remand prisoner from the word go. So far this year he has been subjected to 750 strip searches.' He also said Roderick had made the apparent suicide attempts 'because of the conditions and the way he had been treated'. But no one could explain how he was able to do it.

The previous month Finch had warned the court that the former army officer was 'in danger of going mad. The situation is a dangerous one.' He read to the court from a book on the effects of solitary confinement, which said prisoners were liable either to believe themselves to be going mad or commit suicide. He asked, 'Why was he brought here to prison trussed up like a chicken and placed in solitary confinement?'

Blackburn Gittings, now used to such shock tactics, snapped back: 'Gibraltar's prison is civilized. Take a walk down to Wandsworth or Pentonville any day. I will go with the deputy governor and yourself to inspect the prison. I don't have a magic wand. We could not turn the Moorish castle into the Ritz for Newall's arrival.'

On 11 October, the day the defence finally ran out of legal loopholes to exploit and de Silva started his dramatic opening speech in the extradition hearing, came the final attempt to prevent Roderick being sent back to Jersey. The police van used to take him to and from prison and the court was the most secure vehicle on the Rock. As it stood parked in the yard behind the court in between its police-car escort and with several officers on watch, a surgical knife, still in its hospital wrapping, was found beneath Roderick's seat. It was spotted by Inspector Wink, who was in charge of security during a routine check before the return trip to the castle.

'How it got there I will never know,' said Wink. 'It is just one more mystery in this whole case.'

But the dirty tricks spread further than attempts to aid Roderick to escape or to kill himself. On 19 August 1993, a sophisticated radio listening device was discovered in de Silva's suite, the venue for all the prosecution's legal conferences. The bug was placed behind a picture – a print of a Nelson sea battle in the aptly-named Trafalgar Suite – at the Holiday Inn, now renamed White's Hotel. The device, the size of an old half-crown coin with a loose wire trailing from it, was capable of picking up the details of the legal planning as the Crown drew up its court tactics around the conference table in the spacious suite.

The QC was incensed, but he decided not to make any protest. 'Frankly, we had no idea how it got there. There were many theories as to who might have been responsible. I have handled many cases around the world, but this was by far the most scandalous and underhand trick that I have come across,' he said. 'Exactly twelve months after Roderick's arrest, we had to ask ourselves exactly how much of our discussions and planning had been overheard and our efforts neutralized. This applies to police work as well. We had talked about the general security of all our witnesses, but when it came to Helena Pedo we made doubly sure that our decisions were reached and action co-ordinated at police headquarters.

'No action was possible because we had no proof. We just packed up our papers and adjourned elsewhere until the suite had been given a thorough check for other devices.'

Bug detection equipment was brought to the Rock to give the suite a thorough sweep.

Two days later, on the eve of a vital hearing in the Supreme Court in September 1993, another shadowy figure appeared at the hotel. There was a unique confrontation between de Silva and this man, who cannot be named for legal reasons. The QC delighted in recalling that chance meeting in the lobby. He explained, 'I had met this fellow years ago, when he had some connection with MI6, and I recognized him straight away. I shouted across to him. He turned, and I said to him, "What are you doing here?"'

'He replied: "I am on government business, and you?"'

'I said I was also on government business. With that, he hurriedly left. A check that evening showed that the man had booked in for three days in the room next door to Adamson, but left hurriedly.'

A card this man had handed out, before bumping into de Silva, bore two lines of initials indicating degrees and qualifications. There were also three telephone numbers. None of them proved to be connected lines.

By this time Detective Adamson reported to de Silva that his hotel room had been rifled but nothing stolen, indicating it had not been a common thief but an intruder looking for specific items. This same mystery man was to turn up in Gibraltar yet again as Roderick was waiting for the fifteen-day period allowed for last-minute appeals before being extradited out of the colony to Jersey. This time he had a suitcase stuffed with banknotes – a reported £170,000. He was detained briefly, since it is not an offence to bring cash into the offshore banking haven. But the authorities found cause to hold on to the money for three weeks. By that time Roderick was safely in Jersey prison.

Said de Silva, 'We were always aware, always on our guard, more so after the bug was found and the rooms searched. There is not the slightest doubt in my mind that these dirty tricks concerned Roderick Newall and our attempts to have him extradited to face justice. There seemed to be a lot of money available.'

On 19 July 1993, Finch accused Jersey police of dirty tricks themselves, alleging that a 'mole' in the prison was reporting to them on phone calls made to Roderick. He told the court: 'Under the law, once a person is inside on remand he is out of hearing. Jersey police are playing a dirty game. I believe phone calls to Newall, even those from me, are being tapped and confidential information passed back to Jersey. This is outrageous.

'Jersey has built this case out of all proportion. It is one of alleged grave family aggression, but every time Newall is brought to court he is handcuffed and surrounded by police with shooters.'

Ian Christmas dismissed this allegation: 'It is not a case of grave family aggression, it is one of double murder. There is no informant to the Jersey police inside the prison. The police, in their investigations, have not been outside the law. That is nonsense.'

16

Get Mark

By Christmas 1992 the Crown had won back their lost ground and put the case 'back on the rails'. Roderick had seen his dream of instant freedom fade and his hopes of bail squashed, causing a rare display of courtroom anger when the press sitting just behind him could clearly hear him snapping at Finch, seething with fury, 'I want to see you – now.'

Helena Pedo's statement was not only a 'blockbuster', as one lawyer put it, but was also, unquestionably, admissible in court. The Crown, which had been relying on just the confession in the Dunkeld Hotel, now had two with the clout to put Roderick on an aeroplane to Jersey to face trial.

After a three-day hearing, the Gibraltar Supreme Court ruled that Pizzarello had been wrong to rule the tapes inadmissible. They were now officially back as part of the evidence.

Christmas and the New Year was hardly a festive

time for Roderick, still recovering from his second suicide attempt. Friends had sailed the *Austral Soma* around the coast to Sotogrande, where its name had been painted out and the Red Ensign hauled down, to be replaced by a Spanish flag of courtesy. Roderick's options were either to surrender to extradition straight away, or to fight it all the way in the courts at a fearful cost.

High-powered barrister Brian Leary QC had been brought over from London to argue the defence case in the judicial review. Leary had for many years been a senior prosecution counsel for the Crown and had been known as 'The Gangbuster' in the days when he had helped to bring to justice some major London criminal rings.

One of the principal strands of the defence was a case which became a legal precedent. Leary himself had appeared as counsel in this case, and could therefore speak with authority on it. But his expertise on the admissibility of secretly-taped evidence was costing Roderick an estimated £2,000 a day. By March 1993 his costs had risen to a reported £80,000.

Where was this money coming from? The Crown made no bones about it: the flow of cash was coming from Roderick's younger brother in Paris, who was allowed to talk to him at length once every week. During these calls Roderick was urged not to give up – to keep fighting regardless of the cost.

Throughout his many court appearances, Roderick

was always formal, never once missing the discreet bow of his head in respect to the court before taking his seat. He always carried the latest book he was reading. They ranged from *Zen and the Art of Motorcycle Maintenance* to thrillers. He would listen intently to proceedings, sometimes conferring with his counsel. During intervals, not long enough for him to be taken to the grim little cell in the courthouse patio where, through the grille, he could be seen lounging on a bunk, he often shared a joke with his legal advisers.

Only once was he to show emotion, through all the tedious court appearances, many of which were to last only a few minutes. He surprised court officials by literally stamping his feet in support of Finch's comments that his client had resorted to attempting to harm himself solely because of the horrendous conditions at the prison, where he was being kept in isolation, and the continual strip searches.

Occasionally Roderick would look around the court, particularly at the press gallery, which because of the major interest in the case was temporarily located in the jury box of the Supreme Court, between the bar and the judge's bench. But his attitude throughout was one of superiority, as if all around had nothing to do with him. His former regiment would have been proud of such staunchness in the face of adversity – he was displaying the true bearing of a Royal Green Jackets officer.

By the turn of the year Roderick was aware that the cards were stacked against him and he was forced to give his blessing to the first tentative moves by the defence at plea bargaining, while maintaining the threat of pursuing every possible legal channel to delay the extradition. The authors learned, while in Gibraltar, that Finch approached Attorney General John Blackburn Gittings on the last day of the year with the offer of a deal. On the table in Gittings's office just a few yards up a back street behind the court was the offer: Roderick would consider returning voluntarily to Jersey and pleading guilty to the double murder. He would also show police where the bodies were buried.

But the price of his co-operation was high. He wanted assurance from the Jersey AG that there would be no proceedings against Mark and that he, Roderick, would serve only fifteen years maximum. The Crown was secretly pleased at this first indication that Roderick was showing signs of wanting to finish the matter.

'But there was no way the prosecution could accept any such deal from a man accused of a double murder, trying to set his own prison sentence. You must remember anyway that by this time we were in the driving seat on the legal issues. Optimism had returned and there was a strong belief that he would be brought home to face justice without us having to give anything away,' said a Crown lawyer.

Finch has refused throughout to discuss the case, relying on his often outspoken attacks on the Crown's conduct, in court throughout the fifteen-month legal saga, to represent his views. Even with Roderick long gone from Gibraltar, Finch still refused to break his silence to the authors. The laconic lawyer would say only: 'The confidentiality of what happened between my client and myself must remain sacrosanct. But if I were to talk, it would shake you and the establishment.'

Some observers take that to mean that the lawyer is still totally convinced that Roderick was subjected to unnecessarily harsh conditions with the express purpose of breaking his will and, after losing the first round, the Crown forced through extradition only by means of dirty tricks. Dirty tricks or not – and the Crown has always scoffed at these allegations – de Silva held one more legal ace up his sleeve. He decided that the flow of cash from Paris would have to be stopped. Mark had to be arrested and extradited to Jersey.

The first move came early in February. De Silva told later how Mark's movements were traced through the payments he made on his American Express card. He heard that the broker was planning to move to his bank's New York office. Extradition from the United States can take years, particularly for an astute man like Mark with the funds to stand bail and arrange the best legal defence. The Home Office produced the necessary documents, which Adamson and Marks then took to

Paris. At their office on the third floor of the Brigade Criminelle HQ, overlooking the Seine near the Palais de Justice and Notre Dame, head of the Parish murder squad Odile Fraisse welcomed the detectives.

She is, say French journalists, the most unlikely lady to head such an elite squad of tough detectives. Standing less than five feet tall in her stockings, Mme Fraisse hides behind spectacles and a disarming smile. 'Don't be fooled,' said one Paris crime reporter. 'This lady has worked her way up a man's world on merit and you should not be misled by first impressions. She is tough and has a reputation second to none. I know several detectives in the murder squad, and they have nothing but admiration for her.'

Mme Fraisse wasted no time in taking the two Jersey detectives – as always in the past nine months, CID chief Marks and the ever-present Adamson – to a judge in chambers at the Palais de Justice. She recalled how the judge went through the normal routine of putting into effect the arrest in an extradition request. It would, he said, be carried out by French officers alone; the Jersey officers could be nearby, but not present. However, they could conduct a search under the supervision of their French colleagues and anything taken must be shown to him and documented. The judge also agreed to their request not only that Mark's flat be searched but also his office in the Place du Vendôme.

Tuesday 16 March was going to be Mark's last day

of freedom for many years. Early that morning, the officers had been reinforced by Charles MacDowall, the man who had arrested Roderick. They were met by Mme Fraisse and two detectives outside Mark's apartment block in rue Paul Valéry, close to the Arc de Triomphe.

The French police told later how her men instructed the concierge of the flats to accompany them to Mark's door and, while they hid, to inform him that she had a telegram for him. As soon as he opened the door he was overpowered, pinned to the floor and handcuffed. Her job done, Mme Fraisse summoned the Jersey detectives, who were waiting downstairs in the street. De Silva told of the luxury in which the French and Jersey policemen found Mark was living. The flat had two small trees in the lounge and full-length mirrors on one wall; there was a CD music system and his all-important computer link. The fitted kitchen was well stocked with up-market TV dinners and fast foods. A white-painted spiral staircase led upstairs from the lounge to the master bedroom. There was a fully-furnished study and a spare bedroom, and at the end of the hall a small roof garden.

While Mark remained handcuffed and under guard he told one French officer that he had been 'expecting a visit'. But what really shook detectives, said de Silva, was something they found among the papers on his study desk. It was the bill from the 'last supper' – that candlelit dinner five and a half years before. Said de

Silva, 'I find it quite extraordinary that Mark Newall should have kept it as some sort of memento.'

MacDowall said later, in Gibraltar, that he was so stunned that he did a totally involuntary theatrical double take as he recognized what he had discovered. Sitting at the Crown's favourite lunchtime table, on the restaurant terrace opposite the Gibraltar hotel, the detective said: 'I just don't know why he wanted to keep it. It baffles me.'

Back in Paris, the Jersey detectives also found transcripts of Roderick's taped confession to his uncle and aunt in the Dunkeld Hotel. Mark had asked for them from the defence in Gibraltar, reflecting his manic obsession with his brother's case, which he was financing.

The concierge – one of those eagle-eyed middle-aged ladies famed throughout France – remembers the day the police came for Mark. 'This young gentleman was the last person in the world who I would believe was in trouble with the police. I was totally convinced when they came round to see me that they were going after the wrong man,' said Mme Camerador. 'I almost fainted when he came down in handcuffs and was put in the police car. He was always so polite to me, even though he was very serious and intense. Do you know that at Christmas he suddenly produced a bunch of flowers for me? He was the only one who lived in this block who bothered.'

Mark was driven by the armed French officers to his office at the bank, where another search took place in front of his startled colleagues. Then it was back to police headquarters, where he was later remanded in custody pending the start of extradition proceedings, which would prove to be as smooth as Roderick's were difficult.

Throughout, said the woman police chief, who supervised the operation, Mark's conduct was 'exemplary'. She added that he remained calm and very cool and at no time did he appear surprised that he should be sitting down quietly watching his apartment being thoroughly searched.

The news soon reached Gibraltar. Finch informed Roderick that his brother was also now behind bars, and less than a month later he made another attempt at cutting his wrists. This time, the injuries were minor but when he refused medical attention, he ended up with blood poisoning and had to be sent to hospital.

Back in Paris, Mark decided to refuse to fight the extradition – to the astonishment of people in Jersey, who knew he was spending fortunes funding his brother's fight to avoid it. But some detectives saw this as a typically shrewd ploy to distance himself from the case against his brother.

On 29 April, Martin Fitzgerald and other detectives from Jersey flew to Paris to escort Mark back in a private jet. Fog on the island caused a long delay, but in the early evening the plane touched down and, in handcuffs, Mark was taken to police headquarters and charged with double murder.

In the presence of his lawyer, Le Quesne, he said that he did not wish to make a statement, but pleaded not guilty.

While Mark was now safely back in Jersey, there was still a long legal haul ahead before he could be joined by his brother. The trouble facing the Crown was that there was nowhere near a convincing case in the dossier against Mark for being involved in the murder of his parents. At that time, as de Silva later pointed out, the Crown was convinced that they would have to rely on both of them appearing in the same dock on the same day. The defence, however, was soon to argue in Jersey that Mark be tried separately.

17

The Deal

Having lost out over the admissibility of the taped confession, Roderick's legal team in Gibraltar tried a different approach: Finch accused the Crown of carrying out an illegal arrest, and this time he threatened to fight the issue all the way to the Privy Council. The Privy Council is the highest legal authority for cases concerning the Commonwealth, and Finch knew it would take more than a year before the Newall case would even be considered for a ruling. During that time, the extradition process would be frozen.

The Crown was incensed by this typically robust tactic. De Silva protested to Magistrate Pizzarello on 20 August, 1993: 'The court must protect its own proceedings to avoid what I am going to call a paralysis of the administrative process. This extradition case should go ahead as early as possible. It is unfair to the defendant, it is unfair to the Crown, it is unfair to everyone.'

Outside the court, one prosecution lawyer was even more scathing about the defence tactics: 'They are trying to keep Roderick out of the same dock as Mark, even though they face the same charge. The defence knows that the case against both brothers is based mainly on Roderick's confessions. We know that it is vital that they stand trial at the same time.'

The defence's tactics in Gibraltar were exactly mirrored in Jersey. From Mark's first appearance in court, his lawyer David Le Quesne strove to have the case severed from Roderick's and to get it heard as soon as possible.

Mark had arrived at court handcuffed to DC Charles Canham. Seale Street, outside the police court, was sealed off for his arrival from prison for the brief hearing. That morning, the lawyer issued a statement claiming that his client had co-operated fully with the police throughout their inquiry and kept them informed of his whereabouts. 'He was shocked and distressed to be arrested on an extradition request made by authorities to whom he has always given full co-operation in the past,' added Le Quesne. 'I had been instructed by Mr Newall not to resist extradition but to facilitate and speed up the process, as he wished to return to Jersey immediately to respond to any allegations made against him.'

In September that year Mark's legal team made their major bid to have him stand trial alone. Le

Quesne told the police court in St Helier: 'Justice delayed is justice denied.' He produced an affidavit sworn by Finch in Gibraltar that Roderick's extradition proceedings were 'unlikely' to be concluded until well into 1994. Le Quesne insisted that a single jury in Jersey would have an almost impossible task to judge fairly the two brothers at the same time. He warned that the longer the delay the less likely it was that witnesses would be able to remember events so long ago and that could be prejudicial to Mark.

'His own recollection may also be affected the longer it goes on. A jury could be swayed if he is unable to recollect things which he said in statements six years or more ago,' said Le Quesne.

Crown advocate Cyril Whelan argued that the court had to consider the demands on its time and the escalation of costs if separate trials had to take place. The irony was that the defence in Jersey was using the same arguments to try and speed up proceedings as the Crown was employing in Gibraltar.

On another occasion, Le Quesne claimed that Jersey's legal system was in danger of acting like a Third World totalitarian regime by continuing to delay Mark's trial. In an attack on Jersey's Attorney General Bailhache, he said, 'I have no doubt in my mind that the AG is playing around with court procedures so that the prosecution can give you something to justify a further delay.'

Firing at as many prosecution targets as possible, he caused more eyebrows to be raised in wry amusement by accusing the Crown of causing the delays in Gibraltar. He described as 'a disgraceful allegation' the suggestion, made by the Jersey police legal adviser Christmas, that the defence was alone responsible for the hold-ups on the Rock.

Back in Gibraltar, some followers of the saga were thoroughly confused as the latest legal moves by both the Crown and the defence switched from court to court. Certainly in the magistrate's court Mr Finch appeared to win many points, only to lose them in the higher courts, where de Silva would win the day. But the delays suited the defence. Finch's legal moves seemed endless, when all that de Silva reckoned he needed was an hour to outline the Crown case that would put Roderick on a plane home.

After the taped confession issue, Finch claimed Roderick's arrest was an act of 'modern-day piracy on the high seas'. Claiming the arrest was illegal, he said, 'Why bother with international law if you just send out a gunboat and bring him in?'

By this time sparks between defence and prosecution were spectacular. The de Silva retort was typical: 'It makes no difference whether Newall had been pulled out of the sea on a fish hook or brought in by the tide on a broken-down vessel – once he was in jurisdiction he had been lawfully arrested.'

Even the prison authorities had to be represented in

the Supreme Court in September 1993 by a QC, as Finch pursued the claim that Roderick was held illegally at sea at gunpoint with no food or water and forced to go to Gibraltar against his will. For over six months, the lawyer had attempted to present an image of Roderick languishing in a medieval dungeon, almost naked and freezing in solitary confinement, with strip searches, all under a round-the-clock guard.

In June, his tactics finally succeeded. For the first time in over 300 days the authorities agreed to lift some of the restrictions. Blackburn Gittings, the Rock's AG, said, 'Newall has now been allowed to mix with other prisoners in the television room during the evenings.' Finch's reply was that it was still inhuman to have two guards watching him constantly.

The defence also made much, in the Supreme Court, of a ruling by the Law Lords that a man brought to England from Southern Africa years previously had been extradited illegally because of a strong suggestion of kidnap. This became known as 'the Bennett defence' or, as it was later dubbed by the frustrated Crown lawyers and the many journalists flying in from Britain hoping for a quick conclusion to the case, 'the Gordon Bennett defence' because it dragged on so long in the courts.

When Finch threatened to take the case to the highest authority, de Silva pointed out that only twice in history had such an issue reached the Privy

Council, and on both occasions it had failed. The defence insisted that Roderick was entitled to exhaust all legal avenues and pursue every opening he could in Gibraltar, because he believed there would be 'no more in Jersey, where he felt his case was severely prejudiced'.

This sent more alarm bells ringing for the Crown, because on that very day in October 1993 an Old Bailey judge had thrown out the case against three detectives accused of perjury and conspiracy in the Birmingham Six affair because the massive publicity over the previous twenty years had prejudiced a fair trial. Was this going to be the defence's next line of attack?

De Silva and his team stayed up late poring over the text of the Old Bailey judge's ruling, preparing for a challenge in court next day. In the end the threat did not materialize, because behind-the-scenes activity had suddenly brought the whole extradition case to a climax.

Mr Finch had surprised everyone by suddenly asking the magistrate to consider legal aid for his client, a request that Mr Pizzarello made plain he would be reluctant to grant. There had been a major clash in the Supreme Court between counsel over the questions of costs. De Silva had pointed out that Roderick still had a £200,000 yacht he could sell, adding that the accused was 'a person of substance, a member of the yachting fraternity . . . ' He went on to say that Finch's application for costs was 'simply another way of achieving a further delay'. It was, said the Crown leader, 'delaying the inevitable by the twists and turns, vicissitudes and manoeuvring'.

Against this background, caused by the plugging of the flow of money from Paris after Mark's arrest, the defence made its first move, since December 1992, to restart negotiations over a possible deal.

On Friday, 1 October 1993, Finch took de Silva aside for a quiet word. Roderick, he said, would return to Jersey and plead guilty to the murders. He would take police to where he had buried the bodies and Mark would plead guilty to being an accessory after the fact to the murders. Finch insisted he would want to go to Jersey to ensure that the deal was watertight, with no last-minute backing out.

The Crown lawyers called an immediate conference back at de Silva's hotel suite, now being swept for bugs and other illegal devices. There was a division of opinion, with some officers stressing they were near to getting Roderick on their own terms and refusing any compromise. De Silva was in favour of the deal, and he received the support of some of the Jersey officers. The Jersey Attorney General agreed to consider the offer.

As one lawyer for the Crown said: 'We were being offered one and a half birds in the hand. That, we thought, was far better than having two in the bush.'

By next Wednesday, no agreement had been reached and Finch made an application for judicial review – in other words an appeal – over the legality of Roderick's arrest. This was pressure. The Crown feared that if the review were to be granted, the whole extradition process could drag on for yet another year. And that led to the old fear of Roderick being released from custody on bail, with every opportunity of escaping from Gibraltar. The threat was shortlived: not only did the Supreme Court reject the application and award costs to the Crown; it also ordered that the extradition hearing should start without any further delay.

At the eleventh hour de Silva and Finch thrashed out the final details of the deal and agreement was reached with the authority of the AG in Jersey. For the defence, Le Quesne would travel to Gibraltar that weekend to put his seal on the agreement. The pack of British reporters, lawyers and police trooped from the Supreme Court the few yards across the courthouse lobby to the magistrate's court to hear the Crown open the extradition hearing.

At 11.30 a.m. de Silva rose to his feet and rushed into his opening address before there could be any further delay. Two journalists had been selected by their colleagues to sit at a desk in front of the magistrate's bench to ensure every word was recorded, despite the appalling acoustics. The QC, with a colourful handkerchief cascading out of the top pocket of his jacket, rose to his full height and said, even before the court had settled, 'It is the case for the Crown that Roderick Newall, then an officer in a fashionable regiment, was an assassin of his parents,

Nicholas and Elizabeth Newall, on or about the 10th of October 1987 . . .'

It had taken him fifteen months to utter that opening sentence. But then came groans. Magistrate Pizzarello interrupted, greatly embarrassed, to admit that he could not find his papers. He had been as surprised as anyone that the case had finally started and had left them on the desk in his office. The court clerk made an effort to find them as de Silva resumed his seat once again with a weary air. Finally, the magistrate went off to find them himself.

What was surprising was that Finch had not caused the delay himself. But then only he, de Silva and their closest colleagues knew that a deal had been struck. Ten minutes later, the court assembled again and de Silva was back on his feet, reading his twenty-page summary of the case. Colourful and brilliantly phrased, it contained, the reporters agreed, virtually a headline in every paragraph.

Finch sat silently, sprawled across the desk in front of him, in such marked contrast to the confident man who had given the Crown such a rough ride over the past fifteen months. De Silva said later that he knew the moment he had finally got through to Roderick was when he had quoted that short passage from *Magister Ludi* by Hermann Hesse.

'I turned as I was reading that to look at Roderick and found him nodding his head furiously and smiling. It was as if he knew by heart the part about killing the master, the same passage he had read to Helena Pedo,' said the barrister.

That night it seemed that everyone was delighted, or at least satisfied. The defence had their deal, the Crown had started its case and knew extradition was finally a formality, and the press had their headlines. Even Roderick could not have been too upset at the thought of leaving the Moorish castle and avoiding a second winter there.

But on Monday morning there was still a second or two of drama left to be wrung from the case. Moments before court was due to commence de Silva was summoned to a courtroom office for a final review of the deal with Finch and Le Quesne. Such was the tension that Martin Fitzgerald, sitting with the public, said aloud, 'My heart won't take this.' But back strode de Silva, giving a discreet nod to the detectives, indicating that all the hurdles had been overcome. There was no objection when Finch asked for an adjournment to organize the surrender.

Finch and de Silva went off to cross the Ts and dot the Is on the agreement over lunch. Unfortunately, and painfully for the defence lawyer, he slipped on the wet pavement outside his chambers and in full view of many of the Crown team – and a Channel TV cameraman who filmed his embarrassment – he broke his leg in two places.

Finch had yet again caused a delay – this time unintentionally – and the next moves had to be delayed a week while he recovered from a four-hour operation. He was to make his final bow in the Newall case in style. On 20 October a police van brought him down from the hospital, where his client had been treated so many times, to the courthouse. There he entered the magistrate's court in a wheelchair, and journalists dubbed him, after the paralysed TV detective, 'Ironside of the Rock'.

De Silva could not resist the quip, made in court: 'Mr Finch does not not believe in doing anything by halves' and wished his longstanding rival a speedy recovery. Roderick, who had arrived in court carrying Watergate reporter Bob Woodward's book *The Brethren*, heard his crippled lawyer run up the verbal white flag: 'The defence has no submission to make in the committal of my client, either on the fact or the law. His defence is to be reserved to such times as when he appears in a court in Jersey,' he said.

De Silva, in his final comment on the Newall case in Gibraltar, said, 'The defence consents that there is a case for Roderick Newall to answer in regard to the murders of his parents.' It had cost the Crown an estimated £2.5 million to extradite Roderick from Gibraltar. This was the estimate of Blackburn Gittings who, throughout the fifteen months had, as the Rock's AG, supplied the Gibraltar Parliament with the running total and reported on how much of the bill had to be met by local taxpayers. There was considerable relief among politicians and public that the colony's share of the bill was a relatively small £70,000. The rest of the tab was being picked up by Jersey.

Magistrate Pizzarello ended the saga on the Rock by addressing Roderick: 'I have to tell you that I shall be committing you now to be taken out to Jersey. You have fifteen days to decide whether to appeal to the Supreme Court against my ruling.'

There was to be no appeal; the deal had been done. As one Crown lawyer said: 'At last the defence has conceded to reality.'

Roderick was going home.

One man was missing from the packed courthouse that day to see the finale: Jim Adamson. The detective who had spent six years nailing the brothers had finally allowed himself to take a much-delayed holiday with his wife and son in Florida. He had to learn the news by telephone.

18

The Secret Grave

As the eight-seater Citation jet piloted by Captain Greg Graham levelled out at 30,000 feet over the Iberian peninsula, Louis Wink, sitting opposite Roderick, recalled that not once had his prisoner shown a trace of remorse since he had arrested him on a Gibraltar warrant on 6 August the previous year.

It was now 6 November 1993 and Wink was a happy man. For the last sixteen months, Roderick Newall had dominated his life, causing him sleepless nights. Even after extradition had been granted, he had a constant nightmare for the fifteen-day appeal period that something might happen to his prisoner in the Moorish castle, considering how many alarming lapses of security there had already been in the crumbling gaol.

Although Wink would always remain silent about the performance of his men, it was common knowledge on the Rock that a certain avenue had been exploited to get through to Roderick. So at 7.25 a.m. local time he was a relieved man when he officially handed over custody of the prisoner to Jersey Assistant Chief Officer Paul Marks, who had been promoted from head of CID only a few months previously.

'We went for him for the last time and found that he was looking forward to going back,' said Wink. 'Roderick asked me if I was going with him, and when I said that I was he expressed a hope that I enjoyed my stay in Jersey. He never looked over his shoulder at the prison as we drove to the airport. I think he was genuinely happy that it was all over at last. We had an amicable and even jovial conversation.

'At first our relationship had been very icy. But over a period of time he became more talkative to me and other members of the escort on the trips to court. He would talk about the coming proceedings and make comments like: "Here we go again." I think what changed him was his growing concern for his brother, back in prison in Jersey. Although I never thought Roderick was innocent, he was throughout a very cool and collected man. If you did not know the background, you would never have suspected him.

'I never saw him display any signs of regret, right up to the last time I saw him. It was in the meadow as he took my Jersey colleagues to the area where he had buried the bodies and it didn't affect him at all; he was like a soldier on an exercise.'

As always, Roderick was surrounded by a heavy

escort on board the plane. While he sat next to his lawyer David Le Quesne, the remaining seats were taken by Marks; DS Charles MacDowall, who had brought Mark back from France on a similar flight; Detective Chief Inspector Martin Fitzgerald, who had also been promoted during the investigation; and Sergeant Peter Picot, making up the Jersey contingent. From Gibraltar came Wink and his right-hand man Inspector Eddie Jones, not only as a thank-you for services rendered, but also to broaden their experience.

During much of the two-and-a-half-hour flight to Jersey, Roderick was in deep conversation with David Le Quesne, mostly spent drafting out a statement to clear Mark of any implication in the murders. The lawyer was to release this statement three days later, on the steps of the police courthouse, immediately after Mark had been further remanded.

But the most dramatic development on the flight came some seventy-five minutes after take-off from the Rock. Advocate Le Quesne reached over and gave Marks a tap on the shoulder and passed him a map of Jersey. That map was the prelude to ending the mystery of where the brothers had buried their parents. Roderick had indicated with two small marks on the map the location of the grave on Grève de Lecq hill, the beauty spot on the north coast where he and his brother had spent much of their school holidays.

After studying the map, Marks handed back to the lawyer a much larger-scale version of the island.

Roderick indicated two spots with a more precise location of where the bodies lay. Roderick was fulfilling to the letter his part of the deal made between the defence and the Crown which finally brought to an end the legal saga on Gibraltar.

The plane touched down at 10.07 and taxied to a corner of the small airport, where five police vehicles were waiting, fifty yards from a huge pack of press and TV cameramen restrained behind barriers. They were to see the same cool appearance that Roderick had displayed throughout the Gibraltar episode. He emerged from the plane handcuffed to Fitzgerald and dressed in smart blue blazer, light blue shirt, jeans and brown suede shoes. Over his arm he carried the Sloane Ranger's omnipresent accessory: a dark green waxed Barbour jacket.

By far the most emotional man on the journey home was ACO Marks. During his regular visits to Gibraltar for the long court sessions he had often betrayed the stress signs of his heavy involvement in the case. He would leave the courtroom and prowl like a caged leopard around the entrance to the building, smoking incessantly. He once explained: 'I just cannot stand sitting and listening to this non-stop legal argument, I find it impossible to relax until we get this man home.'

The night before he was to achieve his ambition, he had tossed and turned in his bed at White's Hotel on the Rock, getting up to phone the meteorological office in Jersey for the latest weather forecast. Fog had delayed Mark's extradition flight home from France, and Marks was convinced that with fog threatening the island again Roderick would be held up too. It was only at 5 a.m. that he was finally assured that the flight would go ahead on schedule.

The emotion became too much for the senior detective. He admitted later that, after Roderick had been safely escorted into the interview room at police headquarters in St Helier, he quietly slipped outside to walk alone in the forecourt, his eyes brimming with tears of relief. Even when his boss came across to share the moment with him, Marks rejected his warm embrace of congratulation.

Waiting for Roderick was Jimmy Adamson who, under the terms of the deal, was to lead him off immediately to start the search for the bodies. One constable revealed that there had been a sweep at headquarters to guess in which part of the island the bodies had been buried. Grève de Lecq had always been the firm favourite, followed by the foundations of a recently-constructed golf course clubhouse, Noirmont Common and the sand dunes near Clos de l'Atlantique.

Police had already agreed to lure away the press by holding a news briefing at a school in the early afternoon so that Roderick could be taken to the scene without the media pack in hot pursuit. At the d'Hautree school, ACO Barry Simpson told the press at 2.15 p.m. that Roderick was still being questioned by Adamson in the presence of Le Quesne at police HQ. There was anger among the press when this was discovered to be a deliberate lie, although some admitted that the police's motives had been honourable and the lie justified.

But they soon found out where Roderick had taken police and headed for Grève de Lecq, the beauty spot on the north coast, at the start of a four-day stake-out. Within an hour, police had set up a scene-of-crime mobile unit in the car park of the Moulin de Lecq, a twelfth-century watermill converted into a pub and restaurant. They cordoned off the winding road running from the bay up the valley to St Mary's village leading to holiday spots such as Devil's Hole. Tapes were strung alongside the hedgerow across the grassy valley and deep into the woods, owned by the National Trust, on the far side. The whole site covered an area of about six acres. Somewhere within it was the secret grave.

The incongruously-named Caesar's Palace dance hall, which was normally closed for the out-of-season period, was commandeered for press conferences. And the next-door Lummy's Bar was set up as an ad hoc press centre for the hungry and thirsty hacks keeping watch for developments.

Roderick had stayed an hour, handcuffed to an officer and surrounded by detectives, trying to recall the exact spot where he had buried his parents, with the help of his brother, before dawn on 11 October six years previously. The first of the arriving press, kept well back, saw the murderer concentrate on an area up the bank on the edge of the wood some 200 yards from the old inn. Under scudding clouds and lashed by a bitter wind, the first of the police search teams began their painstaking work with spades.

Up at the rose-tinted Crow's Nest Maureen Ellam could see them digging from her 'den' with its sweeping view of the valley and the cove. It confirmed what she always knew: her best friends' temporary grave had been just a stroll away. She made up her mind then that when the bodies had been found and the meadowland was back to normal she would plant daffodils to mark the lonely spot.

As dusk fell, ACO Simpson called a press conference in the musty atmosphere of the dance hall. Sitting in front of the stage where dust cloths covered the sound equipment, he confirmed what everybody knew: his men were searching to recover the bodies of Nicholas and Elizabeth Newall.

Back at police HQ Roderick was formally charged with his parents' murder by Barry Walsh, the centenier for St Brelade, the town area where the Newalls lived and were murdered, on the south coast. Under Jersey's arcane laws the centeniers, or honorary policemen, are the only ones allowed formally to charge suspects with an offence.

Roderick finished his first day back in Jersey, this time in the comparative comfort of the remand wing of La Moye prison, less than a mile from Clos de l'Atlantique. But at this stage there was to be no immediate reunion with his brother Mark.

The search resumed at first light, but Sunday was to be a long and fruitless day of labour. Adamson and his squad were up before dawn. ACO Simpson announced that a specialist team of search officers had been brought in from the Devon and Cornwall force to assist in the hunt. Others who flew in at the weekend were Home Office pathologist Gyan Fernando and Desmond de Silva, who had swapped his gown and wig for his weekend country wear. The barrister tramped the boggy grass of the valley in wellington boots, tweed trousers tucked in, Barbour jacket, a sporty tie and a wide-brimmed brown felt hat.

The anticipation among the detectives of a quick discovery was shortlived. The scenery has changed dramatically since the night Roderick and Mark had dug the grave. The meadow with a brook running through it had been relandscaped by Jersey's Waterboard into a catchment area and a pumping station. They had also cleared bushes, installed benches, built a children's playground and even introduced ducks and wildfowl. TV and press cameramen were allowed up the closed road to a vantage point overlooking the valley. They were now within 100 yards of the digging, far closer to a sensitive area than any police force on the mainland would have allowed.

The architect of the landscaping was brought in with the original plans and, in a desperate move, police appealed for everyone on the island, including tourists, to scan photograph albums for pictures of the scene as it had been in the 1980s. The authorities were also to break one of the island's strictest laws as a goodwill gesture to the media. The three-hour closing-time regulation on Sundays from 1 p.m. was overlooked as far as Lummy's was concerned.

A generator now powered a series of powerful lights, illuminating the entire scene while uniformed officers kept watch overnight. That night it was a despondent team who trooped back to their cars after spending a hard and fruitless day digging. They were no closer to discovering the bodies, and for the first time there were some detectives who feared Roderick might be bluffing.

The spotlight switched next morning from the meadow and the woods to the centre of St Helier and the police court where the deal struck in Gibraltar unfolded. But this deal was coming under pressure from high-ranking officers, angry that the decision that the murder charge against Mark would be dropped had been taken so prematurely. They were not satisfied that the replacement charge of being an accessory had been agreed even before the bodies were found. Who knows what forensic evidence might be found on the corpses? they argued. Why should a deal struck hundreds of miles away be honoured now that both of the brothers were behind bars in Jersey?

One of the leading hawks was Paul Marks, the second most powerful police officer on the island. Sitting in Lummy's Bar the previous afternoon he had made no bones about his opinion of what had been agreed outside his patch. He bluntly told journalists: 'That agreement in Gibraltar is not worth the paper it is written on.'

This heralded a stark change in atmosphere. Gone was the cordiality which had helped to bind the police together in Gibraltar during the long and frustrating months. Now it was clear that it was slowly being replaced by the serious question of whether the Gibraltar process had been the correct one, and this criticism of plea bargaining was having a damaging effect on those involved in the case.

That Monday morning, Seale Street outside the court was again closed to traffic as Roderick was brought from La Moye in a white police van and emerged to walk swiftly into court handcuffed to an officer. In just a few seconds David Le Quesne had given the *Jersey Evening Post* its bold front-page splash headline: 'Newall pleads guilty.' While Roderick remained silent and expressionless, Le Quesne told the court: 'I am instructed to plead guilty to both charges of murder by my client.' Centenier Walsh had read the charges of two separate murders, each committed 'with Mark Stephen Nelson Newall'.

The whole hearing lasted only two minutes, but the confusion in the press box was to last far longer. Had Roderick now pleaded guilty to killing his parents with Mark participating in the murders? The wording of the charge certainly seemed to indicate this. It was only later that the wording was revealed as irrelevant, a mere formality. Roderick had not implicated Mark, but the press were still well pleased with their story.

Back at Grève de Lecq a mechanical digger had been drafted in, with no success, during daylight hours. But at dusk there was to be a further dramatic development: a moonlit reconstruction of the night the brothers buried their parents. As darkness fell, Roderick was brought back from the prison to the woodland meadow, followed soon after by Attorney General Bailhache. By this time everyone on the island was asking where the bodies were, fuelled by hourly reports on the lack of progress filmed live at the scene by local television.

Roderick seemed eager to help; there was no hint that he was involved in a wild goose chase. At one stage he stood staring thoughtfully at the handful of houses, trying to recapture the scene. He pointed at certain windows and officers were sent to request that those lights be switched on. He turned and walked with his handcuffed escort to the edge of the wood where the day's trenches had been dug. Then he shook his head and strode sixty yards further up the valley to a corner of the field where shrubs were sprouting a few yards from the trees. It was a considerable distance from where the fourteen-strong search team from the mainland had been concentrating their efforts.

Mrs Ellam was almost at the end of her tether at the lack of success. 'I am desperately sad. I pray that the police quickly find the bodies so they can have a decent funeral and hope, please God, that this is the finale and it will be over soon,' she said that night.

19

End of the Hunt

Adamson woke up on Tuesday morning feeling optimistic that the day ahead would see the end of the six-year mystery. The search restarted at dawn and Mark Newall was due to make his remand appearance in court in St Helier, but was the Crown going to drop the murder charge against him, as agreed in Gibraltar, at this first opportunity?

The answer was no. As in every hearing since his extradition, Mark was merely remanded, this time for a week, 'due to certain matters which may take place between now and then', said Le Quesne. This was an obvious reference to the bodies being found and, consequently, the reduced charge of being an accessory to the murders being brought against Mark. Crown Advocate Cyril Whelan told Assistant Magistrate David Trott that the prosecution had no objection to this.

Mark kept up his businesslike appearance by

appearing dressed in a charcoal-grey suit and an immaculate blue-green tie. His eyes never flickered as he stared straight ahead through his round-rimmed spectacles during the brief hearing.

'My client maintains his not guilty plea to the murder charge,' said Le Quesne. But outside court the lawyer was more forthcoming when he astonished reporters by calling an impromptu press conference on the pavement. Still in his formal lace collar, he read out the statement he had drawn up with Roderick on the flight from Gibraltar on the Saturday morning. Roderick Newall, he said, had made a statement under caution to police admitting that he alone had killed his parents. His brother Mark had not been involved in the killings. In response to questions he said that he believed that Roderick was now feeling relieved, having made the statement.

The journalists were amazed that they were hearing more on the pavement than they had in court. It appeared to be a clear case of contempt of court, yet here was an experienced lawyer disclosing a statement from a client facing a murder charge affecting another client on the same charge who had just appeared in court. The situation was so complex that the local press decided not to print the statement after 'consideration of the legal implications and possible prejudicial bearing on future proceedings in the case'.

It also raised the question of a possible conflict of

loyalties for Le Quesne, who was originally the family lawyer for Nicholas and Elizabeth. Now, he was acting on behalf of both brothers, one of whom had pleaded guilty to murdering them and the other who pleaded not guilty. When asked about this he replied: 'I can either represent one of them, both of them, or – what is more likely – neither of them.'

Le Quesne had led the defence of the two brothers while they were in Jersey, had travelled several times to Gibraltar and was in almost daily contact over the extradition moves. He was the first person Roderick demanded to speak to after his arrest on HMS *Argonaut*. He has strong views about the conduct of the police concerning the arrest of both Newalls. He insists that Roderick should have been cautioned before the fateful face-to-face meeting with his uncle and aunt in the Scottish hotel. Detectives give a wry grin whenever they hear *that* argument.

On Mark's case, he is just as critical: 'The prosecution never had a case of murder against him; if they had, why the hell had they not proceeded with it in the past six years? After his arrest he indicated to his counsel in Paris that he wanted to come back immediately and co-operate with the police. The only thing the police had against him was allegedly something Roderick has said in his taped alleged confession, and the law states that the word of one co-accused, said in the absence of the other, cannot be used against the latter.

'It's quite clear that we didn't want them to go on trial together, because if Roderick had, for whatever reason, gone into the witness box and regurgitated something implicating Mark, even though the judge would have intervened to warn the jury to disregard that as evidence against Mark, they would not have been able to put it out of their minds.'

Meanwhile, Adamson hurried from the court back to Grève de Lecq to help supervise the dig. The search squad had abandoned their original site, and were now concentrating on the spot Roderick had indicated the night before. Nigel Blandin, operating the small mechanical digger, had made two parallel trenches within a few yards of each other on the instructions of the Devon and Cornwall experts, but without success. Officers were to tell how the Jersey detective had stood there wondering why a third trench had not been dug, closer to the trees, where earth from the two other trenches had been piled. He was told that the search team had now abandoned the immediate vicinity and were moving off to another site further away.

But Adamson was still interested in this area, and asked them to check it. As the mainland police walked away, one officer told him over his shoulder that if he wanted it done he should do it himself. So he did. He got a ready response from Blandin, who started moving the piled-up earth. When the ground was prepared, the teeth of the digger's arm struck rock, but then further along there was an area of soft soil. The dig commenced watched by just Adamson and PC Mick Robbins.

At 12.20 the press gallery fifty yards away stirred. One of the authors could see, through his binoculars, Adamson peering intently into the hole. Soon, other officers hurried over. Pathologist Gyan Fernando, in overalls and woolly hat, was waist-deep in the hole, his head bent down. Adamson leaned on a shovel. He was to say later that night in the bar of the Grand Hotel, where many senior officers had come to celebrate the end of the long mystery, 'It was the first time that I really felt emotions about the case. I knew we had found Nicholas and Elizabeth as soon as something different appeared to emerge from the soil. That brought it all home to me, why my colleagues and I had continued the investigation for so long.'

It did not need the brief press statement read by Marks, that human remains had been discovered, to confirm the grim find. By that time screens had been erected around the grave, which was covered by a tent.

The detective who had made the first routine inquiries on what was then a missing person's report on that Monday morning in October 1987 had now ended the mystery. All that remained was to disinter the remains of Nicholas and Elizabeth. Both had indeed been buried in the clothes they had been wearing for the birthday dinner. Then, as they lay dead in their home, their bodies had been tightly wrapped like mummies in black plastic sheeting and bound with cord.

That evening, Jersey's newly-formed Territorial Army unit laid temporary metal tracks up the grassy slope for the ambulance to back up to the graveside to take the remains to the hospital mortuary. In La Moye prison the brothers were informed.

Prison governor Keith Wheeler revealed that Roderick and Mark were now allowed to meet and talk during exercise periods. He said that no special arrangements or extra guards had been placed on Roderick, despite his four suicide attempts in Gibraltar.

'We are treating him the same as every other prisoner. The brothers have access to TV, newspapers and the prison library and, like everyone else, have a choice of working in the kitchens, garden or workshops,' he said.

Le Quesne said there was no animosity between the pair, who seemed to be 'behaving with normal brotherly feelings towards each other'.

Senior officers telephoned the news to the closest members of the family: the twin brother of the dead man and the older sister of his wife. Jersey's television programmes were interrupted by Channel, the local ITV company, with a news flash of the discovery. It was also to figure prominently on radio and TV throughout Britain, and make headlines in every national newspaper next day.

Five weeks later, Nan Clark, who had been four years older than her sister Elizabeth, became the first close relative to break the family silence about the tragedy. She told the authors that even after so many years she still suffered a grievous sense of loss. 'You start to get used to it but you can never accept it,' she said in her soft Scottish accent. 'The first moment I was sure that Elizabeth and Nick had been murdered was almost as soon as I arrived in Jersey, after being told by Mark that they were missing. We were in the house when blood was found on the poker. From that moment on, there could be no doubt that they were dead.

'I only gradually became aware that the two boys knew more than what they were saying. It sank into my subconscious and eventually rose to my mind. But I cannot honestly say that I woke up one day and the penny dropped; that is not the way it happened. It just gradually dawned on me that perhaps they were involved.'

Speaking at her daughter's home in Blair Drummond in the Scottish Highlands, not far from the Dunkeld House Hotel, where she was spending a Christmas break with her daughter Amanda, she continued: 'It is all a terrible shock which lives with you and numbs you for a very long time. You have to force your mind to come to terms with it and eliminate any other possible explanation, sifting through everything before you are certain. The final realization that the boys were involved was another terrible shock, even when I half expected it, because I didn't fully admit it to myself.

'You have to divorce the criminal from the crime, particularly when it is family. It is all very hard. I try to remember that the crime is always an awful lot worse than the person who perpetrates it. My sister died; they were her children. I have to have some responsibility towards them.'

She had tried to maintain that family contact when she visited Roderick in Gibraltar, recovering from one of his suicide attempts, even after she knew he had admitted killing his parents to Stephen, her brother-in-law. Mrs Clark had given Roderick a personal letter to read after she had left and he read and reread it night after night, clearly moved. Police were worried to see an important prosecution witness visit the defendant, particularly when she then went to see his lawyer Finch, but they had no need to doubt her integrity. This was just the concern of an aunt for her nephew in poor health.

However, Mrs Clark recognizes that the family will have to live with the tragedy for ever. But her characteristic Scottish pragmatism will not permit herself a second's self-pity. 'I have been brought up to believe that you must jolly well get on with life – regardless of what has happened, even something as truly tragic as this,' she said. 'It is no good thinking about the past and the guilt. Somebody has got to keep going when you have two nephews in prison and a rather frail mother to worry about. You just have to get on with it, and a very good thing that is too. After society has disposed of the problem in its way, the family still has to live with it. That is something we all have to work our way through.'

Mrs Clark has still no idea what motivated Roderick to kill his parents and Mark willingly to help bury them and lie barefacedly to police and family about it afterwards. But she is certain that neither hatred of the parents nor greed for their money could have played any part in it: 'The boys had no great need of money. Mark could make as much as he liked at any time. There was no necessity for him to look elsewhere,' she said. Roderick had a good career ahead of him, not just in the army but, she reveals for the first time, he also had aspirations to become a member of the elite branch of the police: 'He had talked about leaving the army because he wanted to join the anti-terrorist squad of the Met police. Several of his fellow officer friends had already done this and the idea appealed,' she said.

She dismissed any theory that the boys hated their parents: 'They had a perfectly normal upbringing; my sister was always extremely concerned about them and extremely proud of them. Teenage children often have problems with their parents, and vice versa. That is not an unnatural situation – what happened was unnatural, but what I am saying is that the two generations quite often clash.'

She also spoke of the characters of the two boys she knew, although admitting her memories will always be of them and not the grown men they became: 'Roderick was very sociable. He liked people, he was extrovert and very kind in lots of ways. As an aunt I could not have any complaints about such a nephew. Mark was slightly more introverted. As a child, he was happy and lively, but became less so after he went into business, in which he worked fifteen hours a day. It does not leave anyone a great deal of time to socialize. I didn't see a great deal of him when he grew up, but that is often the way between aunts and nephews when they become young men. He would come to family Christmases sometimes.

'Both of them had everything they wanted: skiing holidays, scuba diving, all the water sports, plus the benefits of a good education.'

Of her meeting with Roderick, which was to play such a significant part in the Crown's case, she said, 'I didn't deliberately set out to make him crack. The conversation just came round to the question of his parents naturally. I took the view that what we said to each other was a private family matter and nobody else's business. That is why I did not phone the police immediately. It might have played an important part in his eventual arrest, but I did not view it in any other way than a family discussion. I had not seen Roderick for many years and I was surprised he was back in England at all as he was a young man who liked to travel; all I was trying to do was maintain family contact.'

Unlike Maureen Ellam's two dreams about the victims, Mrs Clark described hers as 'a nightmare that had nothing nice or visionary about it. It was a very peculiar thing which happened, but one of many that take place throughout your life which you cannot explain. I must admit I had forgotten a lot of the details by the time the police asked me for a statement; I was struggling to remember much of it.'

The Crown had insisted in Gibraltar that this nightmare had occurred on the night of 10 October 1987 – the night of the murders – but Mrs Clark now denies this. 'It happened several years before the event; it was certainly not just before Elizabeth was murdered or even more recently. She was warning me about something, but she did not mention Roderick at all.'

She then left in the air the question of who the warning was about, but added carefully, 'I cannot say it was Mark but what I am saying is that it was not Roderick.'

Her belief in family links again surfaced in her complete faith that the extra security measures recommended by the police when Roderick was arrested were completely unnecessary: 'I was not concerned in the slightest for my own personal safety, although my husband Alistair was. But then husbands are usually concerned about their wives, aren't they? I had known the boys forever. I didn't think their approach to me would be a bullet in the back. I thought the extra security was necessary and I went along with it because the police thought it was important.'

20

A Pair of Rice Flails

Roderick and Mark stood side by side, their hands grasped in front of them, as if at morning assembly back at Radley. It was four months later, and the winter chill of November had given way to the first suggestions of spring sunshine.

On 17 March 1994 they were in the dock of the police court for the penultimate chapter of the bloody saga. The committal was to last just forty-five minutes, but for the first time the world was to hear Roderick and Mark's version of why their parents had to die, their bodies to be secretly buried and all evidence destroyed.

Roderick led the way into court from the cells, flanked by burly police officers. The jeans and navy-blue blazer he had worn at virtually every other one of his countless court appearances were replaced by a dark grey double-breasted suit, and a tie dotted with crests. His neatly-combed hair had grown long in prison, far longer than would have been tolerated by his commanding officer in the Green Jackets, and it covered the collar of his light blue shirt. His fit, confident-looking appearance was in stark contrast to that of his brother, who followed him. The months in La Moye prison, amounting almost to a year, had clearly taken its toll on him after his luxury lifestyle in Paris. His identical grey suit hung off his now gaunt frame. He too had shunned the prison barber and his shaggy fringe hung over the frames of his fashionable spectacles, forming a curtain behind which he appeared to want to hide.

The police court itself is attached to the town hall, tucked away down a side street off St Helier's main shopping street. Inside, it is a bemusing clash between one-time colonial splendour and grating 1960s decor. Framed oil paintings by various obscure Jersey artists all in need of restoration hang on lime-green walls. Carved wooden benches and desks stand beneath a mustard ceiling and fluorescent strip lighting.

The public seating was packed with the nation's press and media, including two courtroom artists from TV networks making full use of the opportunity, denied them on the mainland, of sketching in court. Proceedings had begun as usual at 10 a.m. with Assistant Magistrate David Trott dispensing justice to the routine collection of drunks and speeding drivers. It was now 11.15, and the final charges had first to be put to the brothers by Centenier Geoffrey Cornwall.

First, to Mark, he said: 'The said Mark Stephen Nelson Newall with having, between 10 October 1987 and 31 January 1991 in the island of Jersey, knowing that his brother Roderick Innes Nelson Newall had murdered Nicholas Park Newall, criminally assisted the said Roderick Innes Nelson Newall after the commission of the said crime, by assisting in the disposal and burial of the body of the said Nicholas Park Newall, by assisting in the removal, destruction or concealment of the murder weapon or weapons and any other evidence of the commission of the said murder, by making false and dishonest statements and representations and, by the aforesaid acts, assisting the said Roderick Innes Nelson Newall to evade being brought to justice.'

He then read an identical charge, replacing Nicholas's name with Elizabeth's. To each advocate David Le Quesne, sitting behind the brothers, raised himself half to his feet briskly to utter 'Guilty.'

The centenier then read two much shorter charges to Roderick. 'The said Roderick Innes Nelson Newall with having, on or about 10 October 1987, in the island of Jersey, murdered Nicholas Park Newall.'

'Guilty,' said Le Quesne again.

'The said Roderick Innes Nelson Newall with having, on or about 10 October 1987 in the island of Jersey, murdered Elizabeth Newall née Nelson.'

'Guilty,' repeated the advocate.

These were the words that the police and public of

213

the island had been waiting six and a half years to hear, yet strangely not one senior officer was present to witness this drama – neither Chief Officer Bob Le Breton, his at times emotional deputy Paul Marks, nor the head of the uniformed branch Barry Simpson – all previously head of Jersey's CID. Missing too was Detective Inspector Jim Adamson, now to be known under his new title of Police Inspector Adamson.

Like all good dramas, the hearing started off at a snail's pace to mutterings of discontent from the press pack, who quickly started to wonder whether their trip from London would prove a complete waste of time and money. Crown advocate Cyril Whelan told the court that the purpose of the hearing was 'for the prosecution principally to establish a prima facie case against both accused'. He called his first witness, forensic odontologist David Lewin, a friendly-faced scientist, to identify the victims. He was asked to name his qualifications and experience and when, many moments later, he was still detailing his impressive and lengthy academic record Magistrate Trott turned to Whelan and said in mock exasperation: 'I think he has answered that question.'

It provided the one light-hearted moment in the grim catalogue of events that morning. Lewin explained that he was satisfied that the bodies he had examined were those of Nicholas and Elizabeth Newall. He had studied the jaws and teeth of the bodies and compared them with the Newalls' dentistry records. 'The findings were so unique, there was so much data there, that I am satisfied that the remains are those of the people I described,' he said.

The scientist added, 'In the case of the female body, I found that the number of teeth was the same and there were seven fillings. I also found two wires in the jaw where surgery had been performed, which was a dramatic find. There was also one wisdom tooth which had not erupted in life and was very distinct.'

The number of teeth in the male skull also matched Nicholas's dentistry records. 'Twenty teeth had fillings, which is a very high number. The materials of the fillings were consistent with the records, and two dental crowns were in place. There were no inconsistencies.'

The next witness was Home Office forensic pathologist Dr Gyan Fernando, who told how he had been present when the bodies had been found at Grève de Lecq: 'We unearthed what appeared to be a shoe wrapped in a black plastic liner. Further excavation revealed two human bodies, and these were eventually exhumed without disturbing them,' he said. 'We removed them in an archaeological manner. The bodies were fully dressed with all clothes and personal effects and covered in large sheets of tarpaulin.'

He said that he carried out an autopsy on Nicholas on 11 November and on Elizabeth the following day. As Dr Fernando gave the precise details of the violent impact of Roderick's blows on his parents' defenceless

215

heads the brothers sat passionless and expressionless just feet away. Eyes across the court switched to stare at the brothers as the pathologist said: 'In the case of the female skull, there were a series of lacerations on the scalp, seven individual lacerations measuring between five and a half centimetres and one and a half centimetres and extensive fractures of the skull. The injuries I have just described were caused by blows to the head delivered by some other person.'

Turning to Nicholas, he went on: 'Injuries to the male skull were also a series of lacerations. Two of the lacerations were to the front part of the head and the six other ones were present on the back. They measured between eight centimetres and three centimetres. Underlying the lacerations to the back of the skull were extensive fractures of the skull. There were no other injuries to the bodies.'

He told the court that the injuries to both were sufficient to cause death and gave his official cause of death as multiple injuries to the head.

The highest-ranked police officer in court, Detective Inspector Martin Fitzgerald, shifted the focus from the bodies to the brothers. He told the court that he had played a full part in the inquiry since 1987, first in charge of the incident room at police headquarters, and that recently he had become senior investigative officer in charge of the inquiry. The detective described how he had flown to Paris on 30 April 1993 to help in the extradition of Mark and then on

5 November he had gone to Gibraltar and returned the next day with Roderick.

He emphasized how helpful Roderick had been in helping to locate the graves. But for three days they were unable to find them. 'I was present when the mini-JCB digger removed soil, revealing what appeared to be some black polythene. Police officers got into the trench, which was three feet deep, and examined the polythene,' he said. 'It was found to contain a shoe. Excavation continued throughout the day and the following day and it transpired that the shoe was on the foot of Nicholas Newall. His body was wrapped in green tarpaulin and the body of Elizabeth Newall, in the same grave, was wrapped in blue tarpaulin.'

What came next sent the pressmen into overdrive, getting down every word the detective said. 'On 6 November Roderick Newall made a statement to investigating officers,' he said. Martin Fitzgerald read Roderick's very words while the former army officer remained cold-eyed and stony-faced: 'I admit that I killed my parents at 9 Clos de l'Atlantique. My recollection is not completely clear after so much time. The circumstances were that after Mark had left, my parents and I were alone in the house and continued talking and drinking in the sitting room of their home. A heated argument developed in which many old wounds were reopened. It came to a head with my father and I standing face to face and I told him what I thought of him, saying things that I never said before.

'He pushed me and I fell, hitting my head on the dining-room table. I found myself beside a box of possessions which I had sorted out and removed from the attic early that day. On top of this box was a pair of rice flails which I grabbed and used to club my father.'

It was the first time it had been revealed that this lethal martial-arts weapon, of batons joined by link chain, was the murder weapon. Several in the court had never heard of such a weapon, but the whispered words 'kung fu' and 'karate' which sped around the public seating gave a general indication of what it was.

He continued: 'I remember him falling. Next moment I found myself sitting on the floor of the hall. I got up, went into the sitting room and saw my father's body. I could find no pulse. In a complete panic I checked the kitchen and bedroom, where I found my mother's body. This triggered my memory of attacking her and I then realized I had killed both my parents.

'Sometime later I contacted Mark, told him what had happened and said that the only thing to do was to kill myself. He persuaded me not to do that and said he would meet me at the house. When Mark arrived I think I was in the sitting room holding a shotgun. Mark eventually calmed me down and talked me out of taking my life. We then took the bodies in the van and buried them. We returned to the house, possibly via La Falaise, and tried to remove all traces of what had happened.

'My feelings of guilt and remorse built up ever since that night. I found it increasingly hard to live a lie.

'I wanted to help my uncle and aunt to end the uncertainty, but I was worried about the effect on my grandmother of bringing the matter up again. I was particularly concerned for Mark, who had helped and supported me in coming to terms with what I had done. I felt certain that the police would not accept the truth, which was that he was not involved in the killings. Soon after my arrival in Gibraltar I instructed my lawyer to offer that I would return to Jersey if Mark was not prosecuted, but it was made clear that no decision along those lines could be made.

'I have still not understood how I was capable of committing such horrific crimes. I think it was probably caused by bitter childhood memories awakened by the argument. I am relieved that this is all out in the open. I am appalled by what I did to my parents. I am very sorry that Mark is suffering when his only involvement was after the killing to help and protect me.'

The court was hearing for the first time a new side of Roderick. He had never given any outward sign of even the slightest hint of remorse and conscience since his arrest in August 1992. But here he was baring his innermost thoughts and fears. Despite the confession, however, there was still no public display of emotion to match the words of the statement he had made to the police.

The detective had read Roderick's statement at a brisk pace, without pausing, and he passed directly on to Mark's confession. Despite having been in custody almost a year, intriguingly he had given the statement only two days before coming to court.

'On Saturday evening my brother and our parents drank a great deal of alcohol. They drank champagne before dinner and several bottles of wine with the meal. On returning to our parents' house they started on the whisky and began to argue, not violently, about my brother's career and other matters. It was an argument I had heard before. I was sober and I was not interested in it, so I went home.

'Some hours later, in the early hours of the morning, I was contacted by Roderick. He was crying and incoherent and stated he had killed Mother and Father in a drunken row and he was going to kill himself. He kept saying he was sorry.

'I went straight to my parents' house and found Mum and Dad both dead with severe head injuries. My brother had blood on him and was crying, in a distressed state, holding Father's shotgun. There was nobody else in the house. I told my brother the best thing to do was to call the police. He said that he was going to shoot himself. He felt the police would not understand the circumstances. I argued for some time and eventually I agreed to help conceal the crime. It was then and is now my belief that if I had not done this he would have killed himself.

'I found in the boiler room, garage and garden shed tarpaulins, tools and other equipment to clean the house and dispose of the bodies. I helped him to bury the bodies at Grève de Lecq and dispose of the evidence. There were several pairs of rice flails on the floor; Roderick gathered them up and I did not see them again. He said he had cut them up and disposed of them.

'I lied to my family, friends and police to give my brother an alibi and cover up the crime. I am very sorry I did not call the police that morning. I know that I made the wrong decision, but at that time I could not accept the consequences that I feared of taking matters into my own hands and contacting the police.

'I will always bitterly regret the pain, anguish and trouble caused ever since that night.'

At the end of the statement Whelan asked the detective if either of the accused had retracted their statements.

'On the contrary,' said Fitzgerald. 'On reinterviewing on 7 February this year Roderick confirmed to me he had been responsible for setting fire to the evidence that was destroyed at Grève de Lecq after the murders. This included personal items of his mother and father and items used to clean up the house after the murders. He also told me that one of the items found at the scene of the fire could have been a weapon used in the murders.'

Sergeant Charles MacDowall, the officer who had initially arrested both Roderick and Mark and appeared to play a prominent rose in the long investigation, was called and, to the surprise of many, was back in uniform. He formally confirmed that he had witnessed the statements and sat down with a bemused look at the fact that his role in court had lasted only seconds.

The Crown advocate then summarized the evidence and told the magistrate, 'In these circumstances I have no difficulty in submitting to you that a prima facie case has been established in respect of both accused.'

Assistant Magistrate Trott remanded the brothers in custody, telling them that the documents would be rubber-stamped in a few days' time and that they would be sentenced at a higher court at a later date.

The brief court hearing had been made possible by the guilty pleas, which had averted the necessity of calling more than seventy witnesses from around the world. Such a committal would have lasted weeks and cost a staggering amount, to add to the multi-million-pound bill run up over six years, to be paid by the taxpayer. But these statements – so brief in detail, sworn by perjurers and accepted at this stage by the prosecution – posed serious questions.

What were these 'bitter' childhood memories awakened by the drunken argument?

How was a 'hysterical' man who had just killed his parents able, with the help of Mark, to clean up a house and destroy the evidence so successfully?

Why, if 'guilt and remorse built up ever since that night', did the brothers so brazenly resist all the questioning of the police?

Why, if they so 'bitterly regretted the pain, anguish and trouble' they had caused their family, did they claim their inheritance at the first available opportunity?

Was it purely a coincidence that the tarpaulins, the burial tools and the clean-up equipment were so readily to hand?

As the brothers were returned to La Moye prison still awaiting sentence there was considerable consternation among the people of Jersey that these valid questions might never be answered.

21

The Key Questions

The key questions in the Newall case are: Why did Roderick and Mark do it? And: Why did it take more than six years finally to bring them to justice?

Even members of the Newall family and all their close friends remain baffled concerning the answer to this first question. Both brothers gave their versions of events on that dreadful night at the committal hearing through statements read out in a monotone by a police officer. Not once in any of the court hearings has either of them uttered a word; they both sat expressionless and stony-faced throughout.

Despite those statements, many officers and lawyers involved in the case are convinced that the brothers took to prison many secrets about what really happened – not only on the night of the murders, but in the years both before and after. In many ways this seems typical of a British upper-middle-class family's disdain for having the closet doors opened and its skeletons exposed – despite the gravest imaginable charges.

The Newalls were not aristocracy or super-rich, but the boys had titled godparents, were educated at the best of schools and mixed freely with the establishment. Maybe only a psychologist can unlock their minds and solve all these unanswered questions.

The brothers covered the most horrific hours of their lives in brusque statements to the police of just a few hundred words each. 'We then took the bodies in the van and buried them' – just eleven words for Roderick to describe taking the corpses of their father and mother, wrapping them tightly in bundles, carrying them to the van, driving them across the island, throwing them into a field, dragging them to the edge of the wood, digging a three-foot grave then shovelling the earth back on top of them – all under the cover of darkness and fearful of being discovered at any moment.

Can a worse nightmare be imagined? Roderick described it all in eleven words.

Mark stretched his confession to this vital and emotional part of the crime to sixteen words: 'I helped him to bury the bodies at Grève de Lecq and dispose of the evidence.' There was the admission which covered the charges against him – being an accessory to murder and helping to cover up the crimes. Indeed Mark's entire statement of some 370 words would have barely filled a foolscap piece of paper. Yet on examination it is actually a masterpiece of self-defence. For in it he manages three times to claim he got involved solely to save his brother from taking his own life. Where was the similar concern for his dead parents?

'It was then and is now my belief that if I had not done this he [Roderick] would have killed himself.' A few lines later: 'I lied to my family, friends and police to give my brother an alibi and cover up the crime.' Finally: 'I could not accept the consequences that I feared of taking matters into my own hands.'

Such brotherly love . . . but was there really no opportunity for Mark to do the right thing and contact the police over the next six years and spare some of the grief for so many in his family?

So what else can be deduced from what is known from the past six years?

Roderick hinted in court to bitter childhood memories as his motive for murder. But in his two confessions to Uncle Stephen in Scotland and to Helena Pedo in Brazil, he gave no direct explanation, although he did tell his girlfriend about a banging in his head, which he omitted from his police statement.

It is certainly true that he and his parents had consumed a large and varied amount of alcohol on the night of the murders, but were drugs also to blame? Roderick had a longstanding drugs problem, but was that the fatal mix which pushed him over the edge into a spontaneous explosion of violence?

Or was the crime premeditated? Who was the blond man with the German accent and glasses who, despite being identified by the shop assistant, purchased a perfect burial kit at the hardware store in St Helier: spades, cord, plastic sheeting of the same type the bodies were found wrapped in on the day of the murders?

Then there was the van, hired conveniently in the name of Nicholas Newall, the murdered father. Was its sole purpose merely to transfer a mattress and a bed from one home to another that weekend at considerable expense?

After the murders Roderick was panic-stricken and threatening suicide. The sober Mark was at the very least stunned by what he had found at the family bungalow. Was the burial site at Grève de Lecq, where they knew every tree and field, and which contained so many memories and ironies, really selected on the spur of the moment? Or had Roderick already pinpointed this perfect location?

However, if Roderick was lying and this was murder in cold blood, why did an officer, trained to kill, strike in such a messy way, leaving bloodstains as high as the ceiling of the living room? Could his planning have gone wrong? Could he have lost control of the situation?

There is no doubt that the Newall family was not a happy one. The four could not even get through a birthday celebration for a few hours in an elegant restaurant without an argument which attracted the attention of fellow diners. Despite what Nan Clark says about concerned and proud parents and loving children, there is convincing evidence of considerable friction and animosity dating from the boys' earliest schooldays. There is evidence of the parents putting their own interests before their children, humiliating them in public and of cold contempt existing between Mark and his father and angry outbursts between Roderick and his mother. There were visits to the boys at Radley, but when Nicholas and Elizabeth turned up in their camper van and parked it in the school grounds, the boys must have died of shame and embarrassment. Other parents would have stayed at a five-star hotel and arrived in a limousine.

Money was also an important factor. The parents loved living the high life and, despite their sizeable assets there were, inevitably, troughs when spending money was tight. Mark was obsessed with making money and disapproved of their frivolous habits. The cost of the constant stream of drugs was making a dent in a second lieutenant's salary and as soon as Roderick did come into his share of the family inheritance he bought himself a magnificent yacht. The inheritance amounted to an estimated £800,000, a sizeable fortune for Mark, then a young broker starting out on a City career, to invest.

As soon as it was legally possible the brothers had

their parents declared officially dead. The next move, to claim the inheritance, was a formality. Mark must have been aware that his father was in danger of losing heavily in a Lloyd's syndicate, crumbling in the face of monster claims over asbestos. This must have weighed heavily on Roderick's mind. Had he been alive today, Nicholas Newall would have been one of the many names once wealthy but now broke. The inheritance, boosted by the will of Uncle Kenneth on Sark, would have gone down the Lloyd's drain as well.

In the final years of his parents' lives Mark, according to Maureen Ellam, had taken over the management of the family finances, and she tells of the criticisms he made of his father's portfolio which provoked further rows. It is now understood that the Newall family are considering legal steps to deprive Mark and Roderick of the wealth they inherited as a result of the murders.

The answer to the second question of why it took so long initially lies in the sheer disbelief of several senior police officers that the brothers could be involved in such a heinous crime, and the belt-and-braces approach to solving it taken by the island's Attorney General. This was partly due to the lack of experience of major crime on the peaceful holiday island compared with the mainland and to the pressure of getting every detail in place.

The authors soon discovered that a recent murder trial in the late 1980s which resulted in a not guilty verdict had upset the islanders and severely embarrassed the police and the Crown.

The jury verdict, coming halfway through the Newall enquiry, had a serious knock-on effect. The Crown could not afford to go to court again without cast-iron evidence for this high-profile case – the biggest in the island's history. Was this the reason why Attorney General Philip Bailhache was so reluctant to accept the word of two of his experienced officers about the contents of Roderick's four-hour, secretly-taped confession at the Dunkeld House Hotel in Perthshire in the summer of 1992?

One of Britain's leading psychologists, who normally appears for the defence in major trials, described Roderick's words as one of the most genuine confessions to murder he had ever heard. But the authors were to learn, from Crown lawyers, within months of Roderick's arrest and imprisonment in Gibraltar, that it took three days for an arrest warrant to be issued. This was one of the reasons why Jersey had to ask the Royal Navy, at huge expense, to put a frigate and a fast patrol craft to sea to detain him. This, in turn, again at colossal expense, led to fifteen months of legal wrangling before he could even be brought back to Jersey.

Mr Bailhache, displaying in our opinion his over-cautious attitude, would not issue a warrant until he had carefully studied the contents of the tapes. Detectives Paul Marks, then head of the island's CID, and Detective Jim Adamson must have told him of the explosive conclusive evidence on the tapes. Even though Roderick had given the police the slip on the M6, had a warrant been issued within twenty-four hours and a general alert raised, he could have been detained at a Channel port as he made his way to France. It emerged in Gibraltar that Bailhache had not reached the mainland to listen to the tapes until more than twenty-four hours after Roderick had made his confession to his uncle and aunt on Tuesday, 14 July. It was not until Friday, 17 July that the warrant was finally issued in Jersey and Roderick's name and description circulated throughout Britain.

Over the years the CID had twice compiled dossiers which they considered contained sufficient evidence for the arrest of both Roderick and Mark for murder. But, rightly, the Attorney General's office rejected them on the grounds they were based on circumstantial evidence. Only Bailhache knows whether his caution was a result of the thin case presented on those two previous occasions. Certainly there appears to be a lack of confidence between the Attorney's office and the CID.

Our opinion on this lack of action is supported by the views of Gibraltar's Attorney General John Blackburn Gittings, who stresses he has no brief to criticize the Jersey police. Blackburn Gittings, a former experienced and respected criminal lawyer in London, said: 'I truly believe that had this been a murder in similar circumstances in Britain both brothers' feet would not have touched the ground following the initial complaint to police. They would have been pulled in and they would have cracked and it would have been all over.'

Blackburn Gittings believes that a major shortcoming was the Jersey police's lack of experience in handling a major case on their patch, which is normally law-abiding. He asks: 'Why wasn't Scotland Yard called in at an early stage? I am amazed. There are blokes at the Yard who live with a bag packed, available to travel anywhere at short notice. We all know, those of us who have been in the game, that 90 per cent of such crimes are domestic. It always has been so. You do get serial killers and nutters, but by and large it is domestic. Their hire van was spotted in the early morning and later they were asking neighbours where they could burn rubbish.'

However, he is quick to praise Marks and Adamson as 'very good detectives' and adds: 'Maybe it is much to the credit of the Jersey police that they behaved the way they did, and brought no unfair pressure.'

Jersey police were to go to extreme lenths to bring the Newalls to justice, calling on the help of some of Britain's leading experts in forensic science. One such expert even took the wallpaper and ceiling of the lounge in the murder house back to England with him for examination. But all this might have been unnecessary if Jersey's own scene-of-crime officers had been experienced enough to detect the thin sprays of blood which had escaped the brothers' washing-down operation. True, they were tiny particles on dark surfaces, but an experienced officer would have been expected to find such evidence – another good reason for calling in Scotland Yard straight away.

When Home Officer forensic scientist David Northcott was finally brought in and discovered the two murder scenes, seventeen vital days had gone by since the couple had been reported missing. The brothers' confidence in their cover story must, by then, have grown considerably.

In fairness, at that time there was no hard evidence linking the brothers to the crime. Mark and Roderick had concocted a solid cover story and although their attitude and behaviour was highly suspicious they did not crack once through long hours of questioning. Detectives such as Nimmo, Adamson and Fitzgerald were almost convinced from day one that the brothers were involved in the "disappearance" of their parents, but they appeared not to have the full support of their senior colleagues. They could not come to terms with the concept that in such a peaceful environment as Jersey, two educated, clean-cut sons of an upper-middle-class family, both making progress in promising careers, one in the army, the other in the City, could possibly be involved. One slaughtering their parents and the other helping to cover up the crime.

Maureen Ellam, the closest friend the victims had in

Jersey, vividly recalls Bob Le Breton, then head of CID
and now the Chief Officer of the States of Jersey Police,
and a senior colleague, Martin Le Brock, visiting the
Crow's Nest within days of the murders. 'I did not
know them then, they were in plain clothes, charming
and very polite. My husband David and I made them
tea and all four of us sat in the sitting room,' she said. 'I
told them that although we hated to say it, we believed
the boys knew something about it all.

' "Oh come on now," was their reaction; they could
not believe it. That was one of the main reasons the
case did not get off the ground quickly enough.'

The fluent and articulate Mrs Ellam is, to some who
don't know her, an opinionated chatterbox. Such a
characterization is totally unfair. She was a vital
stimulus to the police to keep the enquiry going,
particularly in the late 1980s when many were
prepared to let it rest on the files. Her shrewd
observations have been totally vindicated. She has
been praised by police as a 'remarkable woman', and
her value to the officers in charge of the day-to-day
running of the enquiry is reflected in the fact that
mainland detectives brought in to help were taken to
talk to her. Marks brought an FBI expert in tracing
buried bodies to see her and he came away convinced
that her opinion was correct. Desmond de Silva QC
had it right when he described her as a sort of 'Miss
Marple'. She too has praise for the footsoldiers,
Nimmo, Adamson and Fitzgerald, and her

condemnation of initial complacency among their superiors is supported by Nan Clark.

The elder sister of Elizabeth Newall said, 'There has been criticism of the police for not detecting the minute blood splashes around the house quicker. But Graham Nimmo and Jim Adamson found the bloodspot on the poker straight away and they could not be blamed. If there are people to be criticized you have to look higher up. There, there was no great interest in pursuing the case. I don't know why. Maybe it was because my sister and her husband were not native islanders. They had been there an awful long time, nearly twenty years, but there is a wide difference between being a real islander and someone who has come in. Detectives on the case at ground level, like Adamson and Nimmo, knew from the beginning that this was serious but it was not the same further up. They were very hesitant.'

Indeed it was another member of the tragic family who played the major role in cracking the case: Stephen Newall, Nicholas's identical twin brother, whose patience and skill drew out the crucial confession from Roderick which hours of police questioning had failed to achieve. This is a fact which, with no false modesty, he recognizes: 'Without my contribution there would have been no case,' he says.

The deal agreed in Gibraltar by which Roderick would plead guilty to the murders, take police to the bodies and Mark would face only accessory to murder and cover-up charges, was the only way to halt the ludicrously expensive legal wrangling. There was no hard evidence implicating Mark in the murders. But what his version of events fails to fully explain is his reaction to receiving the panic stricken phone call from Roderick on the night of the murder. Mum and Dad battered to death! Urge his brother to go to the police or to call them himself? No, he drove over to Clos de l'Atlantique in the van that had been hired the previous day and then embarked on an elaborate and clinical cover-up, first helping to parcel up the blood-soaked corpses, then loading them in the van, driving to the burial site, digging a grave and then returning to spend hours washing down and scrubbing away the evidence.

Despite the fact that the deal produced two guilty pleas and brought Roderick back to Jersey when his legal fight against extradition could have lasted up to another year, it has sparked reports of a rift in the upper ranks of the Jersey police force and the Crown legal office. The team spirit and goodwill that existed in Gibraltar turned sour back in Jersey. While the argument raged behind closed doors, the officers involved in the case were banned from speaking about the investigation to journalists, even those they had come to know and trust for many months.

We believe that the Gibraltar deal became such a hot potato back in Jersey that the authorities did not want any details of the split to become public. They overreacted and imposed a blanket ban on information about the enquiry. Later some could not wait to claim credit. The media blackout imposed in December 1993 was yet another example of the lack of experience in the island when dealing with a major police inquiry of huge interest to the public. The trust in Gibraltar had turned to suspicion in Jersey.

Once the guilty pleas had been lodged, there was an air of discontent around headquarters in Rouge Bouillon. To many, this was strange. A sense of triumph and achievement would have been more appropriate.

The Newall case has been the most costly manhunt in Jersey history. The legal fees have been staggering. QCs like Desmond de Silva command the highest fees. The Crown legal team in Gibraltar and the back-up staff of Jersey detectives almost became residents of the Rock. The bulk of the cost of guarding Roderick around the clock by Gibraltar's firearm squad was picked up by Jersey. There were hundreds of thousands of air miles involved – to London, Paris, Scotland, Miami, Brazil, Spain and the Falklands, not to mention the constant stream of business-class seats taken up on the Gibraltar run. The estimate of the cost of hiring the frigate HMS *Argonaut* and the patrol boat HMS *Ranger* was in the region of £250,000. The documents and affidavits and other legal requirements occupied hundreds of man hours.

Gibraltar Attorney General John Blackburn Gittings estimates the figure to be met by the Jersey taxpayer at some £2.5 million. But this does not include the cost of the six years of investigation on the island before the focus switched to the Rock. At one stage the police budget had to be injected with extra funds from the state coffers.

If only for this huge financial burden, the people of Jersey deserve a full and detailed explanation not only about Roderick and Mark's motives, but also about the handling of the entire case. Could this be a case for an enquiry by a mainland police force into the process of decision-making and the conduct of the investigation?

The Newall case has many similarities to another long-running cliff-hanging manhunt in Jersey in the 1960s. Then, Edward Paisnel, a well-known son of a landowner, conducted a reign of terror, kidnapping young children from their homes and sexually assaulting them while wearing a hideous rubber mask and nail-studded bracelets. He became known as the Beast of Jersey. During that investigation virtually every male on the island was questioned, including Paisnel. In those days there was no genetic fingerprinting and he was caught only because he jumped a red light when a police car happened to be on the spot. He later confessed. Like Roderick, he was sentenced to life imprisonment. That was in 1971, and today he is free and living on the mainland, too frightened to return to the island.

22

The End of the Road

On August 8 1994 Roderick and Mark Newall finally paid the price for their most terrible of crimes.

Jersey's highest court is a colourful one. Ten jurats, who are distinguished members of the island's society, filed past dressed in scarlet and black edged robes. With their historic red, French-style hats they made an impressive sight. The jurats flanked Jersey's Bailiff, Sir Peter Crill, who was dressed in similar garb. His ermine collar and cuffs denote his rank, at the peak of the island's legal system.

Almost unnoticed, the brothers were brought in through a side door at the back of the court. The long hair they sported at committal in the Spring had been neatly trimmed, but they still wore their familiar dark suits and sober ties.

As before Roderick showed a soldier's respect to authority by bowing his head to the Bailiff. Bespectacled Mark made no such gesture. A brief whispered conversation with their advocat, David Le Quesne, followed.

The island's recently appointed Attorney General, handsome fair haired Michael Birt, opened the case with a long review of events from the time that Nicholas Newall, his wife Elizabeth and their two sons had set sail from their native Scotland to begin a new life in the West Indies but settled, instead, in Jersey. It was not until the second hour of his address that he reached the nub of his argument. Roderick had killed his parents, not in a moment of anger as he had always claimed, but as a result of a carefully orchestrated plan.

First he highlighted the blond haired man who has never been identified who, for cash, had purchased the "murder and burial kit" from local ironmongers, Normans, on the day of the murders. The equipment included tarpaulins identical to those used to wrap up the bodies. The shop had only sold two tarpaulins up to the day of the murders. The first was traced, the second was sold to the young fair haired man. Nicholas had two accounts at Normans, but had not bought these items.

"The Crown says that there is considerable evidence to suggest that the purchaser of these items was indeed Roderick Newall," Mr. Birt told the court.

A pick axe had also been purchased at the same time. Forensic examination of the bodies showed that Nicholas was felled with two blows to the front of the head from a heavy weapon, followed by six strikes to the back of the head with a sharp instrument.

This proved, said the Attorney General, that Roderick continued to lie. His claims that the rice flail, which was conveniently at hand, was the only murder weapon were clearly untrue.

This second murder weapon has never been found. But the pick axe sold to the fair haired man had an eight centimetre blade – exactly the same length as the wounds on the back of the skull.

What is more, added the Attorney General, Roderick had admitted being in the vicinity when the purchase was made at 11am that Saturday morning.

Even though the Crown admitted that Roderick and his parents had drunk a huge amount of alcohol that night – three bottles of champagne, three bottles of wine, liquers and whisky – drunkenness had played no part in the murders.

Mr Birt read out a short extract from Roderick's taped confession to his Uncle Stephen:

Stephen: "What about some mitigating circumstances, you know, like a crazy drunken rage or something. Does that mitigate your internal thing as well?"

Roderick: "No."

Stephen: "Well if you . . . "

Roderick: "That was not involved. I mean from the point of view of going to court then, yes, one could."

Said Mr Birt: "Roderick is now indeed 'going to

243

court'. Is he now doing what he there previewed, namely suggesting that the killings occurred in a 'crazy, drunken rage or something' when the truth was, as he indicated to Stephen, different?

"For these reasons, the Crown is unable to accept that Roderick has been truthful. He has lied consistently throughout this investigation and the Crown says that, even now, he can not bring himself to face the whole truth, namely that, at some time before 11am on Saturday October 10 he decided to murder his mother and father."

As he spoke, Roderick sitting just a few yards away shook his head – his first and only show of emotion.

Now in full flow, and with the rapt attention of the entire court, the Attorney General said Roderick had pleaded guilty "to murdering both his parents by bludgeoning them to death in their own home.

"He has offered no explanation of his actions save to say that a heated argument developed, in which many old wounds were reopened. The Crown says there is strong evidence to suggest that the murders did not occur on the spur of the moment as he suggested.

"Whether they did or not, he struck his father repeatedly on the head while he was lying stunned or unconscious on the ground. He used a heavy weapon with a cutting edge. It was a scene of considerable violence.

"He also struck his mother repeatedly on the head

with sufficient force to kill her, when she too must have been lying on the ground. For this he used a single weapon."

Looking up, he added: "It was a terrible crime."

Turning to Mark and his "chilling and shameful part in this tragedy" Mr Birt listed the younger brother's crimes.

"He helped him wrap up the bodies in the tarpaulins, transport them in the dead of night to Grève de Lecq, carry them over 100 metres and then dig a grave to hide both bodies."

He then returned with Roderick to the house to remove "all traces of the terrible crime which had taken place" including the weapon or weapons. Then he continued to lie: They did not have breakfast at their parents' bungalow the morning afterwards. They did not find their parents asleep in bed. They did not leave the house and return to a cosy family Sunday morning reading Sunday newspapers and sharing Sunday lunch.

"Mark's statement in support of Roderick was an intricate and deliberate lie, woven to establish a consistent story so as to provide Roderick Newall with a false alibi."

He continued the cover-up by lying to the police and, in the Autumn of 1990, he lied in sworn affidavits in order to have his parents declared officially dead to inherit their wealth.

"Indeed if Roderick had not confessed to his uncle,

Mark's conduct might well have resulted in no-one being brought to justice for the murder."

He demanded the mandatory life sentence for Roderick, and six years imprisonment for Mark.

David Le Quesne has looked after the affairs of the Newall family for most of his legal career. A member of a prominent Jersey family, the still young-looking advocat was quick to dispel any notion that the brothers planned to reveal their own account of family hate.

"The court has heard little from the Crown about the family background beyond the statement that the relationship between the boys and their parents was 'cold and complex'," he said.

Pressmen exchanged glances of disappointment as Le Quesne continued that his clients had ordered him "not to speak ill of the dead."

"I have been specifically instructed not to attempt to excuse Roderick Newall for his crimes by indulging in character assassination of the deceased," he added.

"He accepts that his crimes are inexcusable. However, I think I can say firstly that such crimes do not occur in normal happy families; and secondly that perhaps some insight into the background of this case may be gleaned from a remark of Stephen Newall.

"I refer to the family conversation in Scotland which, in the absence of any other evidence, provided the reason for the arrests in this case.

"Stephen said: 'we of course watched from

the sidelines and saw two very badly treated little boys . . . '"

Le Quesne denied that Roderick was the fair haired mystery man at the hardwear store and insisted that only one murder weapon was used – a metal tipped homemade rice flail, which was capable of inflicting all the injuries.

Turning to his other client he concentrated on the mental turmoil Mark had faced that night.

"A snap decision had to be made by this young man: help his brother, or call the police. There was no half way point, because if he did not help, his brother was clearly going to shoot himself," he said.

"Once he had taken the wrong decision, which was to help, the tragedy was into its second act. There was no turning back, for to have helped his brother that night and told the police the next day would have been treachery. Once he and his brother had applied their undoubted intelligence to covering the crime, Mark was himself too involved to draw back. His life was on the edge of an abyss. And he knew that at any moment the storm might break."

"Whether Mark's decision would have been different had he been contemplating covering up the murders of two parents whom he loved and respected is a matter for speculation.

"The fact that there was no such love and respect in either direction makes his decision easier to understand. Since then, not only has he had to live with the threat to his freedom but also with the knowledge that many, including his family, had labelled him a murderer."

Then the advocat claimed "this is not a crime for personal gain, this is not a crime of violence."

Le Quesne asked the court to be "just and merciful" and impose a sentence on Mark of no more than three years.

Less than half an hour later the court reconvened. The two defendants were brought back and, flanked by three uniformed policemen, stood just feet away in front of the Bailiff.

Sir Peter Crill wasted few words. "Roderick Newall, you have pleaded guilty to the crimes of double murder," he intoned.

"They were particularly nasty killings. Throughout the ages the crimes of patricide and matricide have attracted particular odium. This court shares that view but, because the sentence I am about to pronounce is mandatory, the court felt it is not necessary to decide whether the murders were premeditated or not.

"You have accepted that your crimes are inexcusable, and so they were. You are sentenced to concurrent life sentences."

Roderick bowed his head and stared at his feet.

"Mark Newall, you too have pleaded guilty to two serious crimes but not of the gravity of those committed by your older brother," the Bailiff continued.

"The obstruction of justice is a serious matter. If you

did not intend to be disloyal to your brother you could have kept quiet, but you went further.

"You made false statements to the police, you assisted in burning the evidence and you provided a false alibi for Roderick, and kept it up between 1987 and 1991.

"The court accepts that without your active support it is probable that Roderick could not have delayed extradition for as long as he did from Gibraltar. It is the view of the court by a majority that the proper sentence is one of six years concurrent."

Sir Peter then revealed that three of his jurats had wanted a longer sentence but had been outvoted.

The brothers were led out into the bright afternoon sunshine, past the jeering crowd, and driven to La Moye prison. Their seven year fight to escape justice was over.

The brothers had left the scene, without any mention of an extraordinary – and previously secret – new twist to this terrible story.

Police knew that Nicholas Newall appeared to have been secretly drugged on the night of his death. Traces of phenobarbitone had been found in his body during a post mortem. No mention of this finding had been made in court because of a dispute between the defence and Crown experts.

However, there was no reason whatsoever for Mr. Newall to deliberately take phenobarbitone – a drug normally used for treatment of epilepsy. It was also a fact that mixing phenobarbitone with alcohol could rapidly precipitate death.

The police believed that, if this evidence had been admitted, it might well have proved once and for all that the killings were premeditated.

The authors also learned that Jersey detectives had re-examined the curious death of Uncle Kenneth.

The dwarf-like, reclusive near-millionaire, Roderick's great uncle, had suffered a massive heart attack after being electrocuted in his bath in November 1987 just a few weeks after Roderick butchered his parents.

Some officers were now considering the possibility that Roderick might have had a hand in what was at first dismissed as a freak accident.

The 75 year old lived on the tiny Channel Island of Sark. A month before the murders the family gathered to persuade Kenneth to place his fortune into a trust fund, to be shared between his two nephews Stephen and Nicholas.

Kenneth was certified officially dead from natural causes and was cremated before the murder hunt officers on Jersey even knew he had passed on. They would have been keenly interested in the death because Kenneth's legacy to the brothers doubled.

Said one detective: "Uncle Kenneth's money doubled the brothers' inheritance, which was ample reason for Roderick to murder him.

"We also think Kenneth might have got a whiff of Roderick's increasing involvement in drugs. We tried to take a long look at the death, but we could not prove that Roderick had been on Sark that day.

"However, anyone who is capable of killing his parents in such a ruthless fashion has to be suspected if another relative he cared even less about died in strange circumstances."

Further doubts must have been raised in the minds of the police by the reported comments of Douglas Newall, a cousin, the day after sentencing.

He was quoted as saying that Kenneth suspected Roderick had used his father's yacht for drug running.

"The story seems to have come from Kenneth before he died. He was approached by Roderick, who had around £300,000 which he asked his uncle to look after," he said.

"Ken agreed to do so, though he believed it was drug money. He relayed his concern to Nicholas and they had a meeting at which the money was handed over.

"Some of us believe that Nicholas then refused to hand back the cash, and that is why the argument exploded."

As Paul Marks said: "Whatever the truth, only four people know and two of them are dead."

Clearly money was at the core of the Newall tragedy. The dead parents loved to spend it, the obsessive Mark loved to hoard and invest it, and the murderer Roderick desperately needed it to live the life of a gentleman of leisure.

But where is this money that the brothers inherited?

Police believe it is growing daily in a myriad of foreign bank accounts and investments, and ruefully accept that a financial wizard like Mark could comfortably hide it forever. Only he would know the codes and the complexities.

Stephen Newall, as head of the family clan, and Nancy Clark have launched legal proceedings to try to recover what they can from the hidden fortune, which is now estimated to be several million pounds.

One detective pointed out that the relatives would have to take court action in every country where it is deposited. It is expected that all they will be able to win is the £110,000 house at 9 Clos de l'Atlantique – the murder scene.

For one young woman, however, the nightmare is still not over. Helena Pedo, Roderick's former lover, has been under police protection in Sao Paulo, Brazil, since giving damning information to the murder squad in the Autumn of 1992.

On the night the brothers were sentenced the fear had still not dissipated, and she told the authors "they should throw away the key to their cells."

The strain and emotion were clear in her voice as she added: "Of course I am still scared. I know they have lots of money hidden around the world, which can employ powerful lawyers.

"But I am more afraid of Mark than Roderick. I think he is more dangerous because he has never said anything. He has never spoken about what happened to his parents to anyone, except for that short statement to police. Roderick seemed to have wanted to get rid of his guilt."

Her two most abiding memories of the man she loved, yet never really knew or understood, were the first and the last time she ever saw him.

"The first time I was in the bar at the marina club with my friend Eloisa when he walked in from the sea looking like a Viking," she said.

"Eloisa pointed him out and said 'let's check him out'. I fell for him. I will always think of him like that, the Viking in my life.

"The last time I saw him was at Miami airport. He was flying back to Britain to buy a new yacht. I never thought for a moment that I would never see him again.

"He checked in, I went with him to the departure gate, he presented his boarding card, we kissed goodbye, he walked down the corridor to the departure lounge . . . he never looked back, he never turned, he never waved.

"That was then, but now the only reason I ever want to see him again is to look into his eyes and get him to say 'sorry'. He put me in a terrible position, I was in despair for me and my children. It is not fair what he has done to us . . ."

But perhaps, in time, Helena will be consoled by the thought that she is luckier than three other people who were once close to Roderick Newall. She, after all, is still alive . . .